Examining the Evidence

Seven Strategies for Teaching with Primary Sources

Hilary Mac Austin and Kathleen Thompson

Foreword by Sam Wineburg

Maupin House by

capstone
professional

Examining the Evidence:
Seven Strategies for Teaching with Primary Sources

By Hilary Mac Austin and Kathleen Thompson

Cover Design: Sarah Bennett

Book Design: Jodi Pedersen

Library of Congress Cataloging-in-Publication Data
Cataloging-in-publication information is on file with the Library of Congress.

978-1-62521-630-4

Maupin House publishes professional resources for K–12 educators. Contact us for tailored, in-school training or to schedule an author for a workshop or conference.

Visit www.maupinhouse.com for free lesson plan downloads.

Maupin House Publishing, Inc. by Capstone Professional
1710 Roe Crest Drive
North Mankato, MN 56003
www.maupinhouse.com
888-262-6135
info.maupinhouse.com

Printed in the United States of America in Eau Claire, Wisconsin
042014   008152

We dedicate this book to two
of our favorite teachers,
Pat Cotter and Bobbi Kidder.

We would like to acknowledge Lynnette Brent for her enthusiasm
and vision, Karen Soll for her insightful editing and keen eye,
our readers—Michael Nowak, Kathleen Cantone, Lindsay Richardson,
and Craig Austin—for their grasp of the big picture and their
attention to detail, and L. Blair Hoyt and Viola Wofford for
working together to get us the Edward Hoyt photo.
And we want to thank Sam Wineburg.

Table of Contents

Foreword by Sam Wineburg 6

Introduction This Is Not *Just* a Photograph 8

Chapter One Primary Sources in History 22

Chapter Two Primary Sources and the World Around Us 32

Chapter Three Strategy 1: Decide What You're Looking at 41

Chapter Four Strategy 2: Determine the Purpose and Audience 54

Chapter Five Strategy 3: Look for Bias 67

Chapter Six Strategy 4: Examine Closely the Source Itself 81

Chapter Seven Strategy 5: Find More Information 93

Chapter Eight Strategy 6: Consider Your Own Role in the Interaction . . 110

Chapter Nine Strategy 7: Compare a Variety of Sources 117

Chapter Ten Apply the Strategies 125

Chapter Eleven Find Primary Sources 142

Text References 153

Appendix One Major Visual Collections 157

Appendix Two A Brief History of Image and Sound Technology 161

Foreword

In August 2005, in the wake of Hurricane Katrina, two photos appeared on the Yahoo News website showing flood-ravaged citizens grasping food and drink as they navigated waters that poured into the streets of New Orleans. The caption accompanying one read: "two residents wade through chest-deep waters after finding bread and soda from a local grocery store." The second photo depicted a similar scene. It showed a man wading through waters, also appearing to hold sodas under one arm and a garbage bag, presumably with food in it, in the other. But rather than "finding" such items, the man is described as having come by them after "looting" a store.

The photos are uncannily similar. Each depicts desperate people grasping items in the most dire of circumstances. Yet, in one case, the captions tell us, these people "found" these items; in the other, a man "looted" them. In one respect only are the photos markedly different. In one, the people are White; in the other, Black. I'll let you guess which caption accompanies which. [i]

Images and words. Neither is innocent. Both shape our thinking, urging us to believe one thing and not another, solidifying our stereotypes or, more rarely, confronting them. Like Katrina's waters, there's no escaping the flood of messages flowing into the nooks and crannies of our consciousness. They beckon to us from the laptop in our backpack, from the iPad on our nightstand, from the smartphone buzzing in our pocket. They call to us to buy something, to support something, to oppose something, to sign something, to tweet something, or to "Like" something. We are up to our neck in messages telling us what to do and think. Without the ability to interrogate these messages, we are destined to sleep walk through our world, blithely accepting without question that what makes one a "finder" or a "looter" is the color of one's skin.

On one level, the book you are holding is about the reading of primary sources. But on a much deeper level, you are holding a manual for citizenship. This book is a guide for awakening tomorrow's citizens to the world they inhabit. *Examining the Evidence* rightfully dissolves the distinction between image and word in our digital society, where both can be twisted, retouched, ripped from one context and slotted into another, used to incite or quell depending on predetermined aims. This book's seven strategies sound an alarm that awakens us and our digital world. How should we start? We begin by paying attention. Next, we ask questions.

Unlike other books that ostensibly promote the new Common Core State Standards, the questions of this book refuse pat answers. Looking at the iconic photograph of "migrant mother" (p. 76), we ask about Dorothea Lange's motivations in serving a program that, according to fellow Farm Security Administration photographer Arthur Rothstein, sought "to document the problems of the Depression so that we could justify New Deal legislation that was designed to alleviate them." [ii] But does knowing the motivation behind Lange's photo, does knowing that it is one of a series of six, each one progressively zeroing in on the subject to achieve the right pose, diminish the emotion, the weather-beaten grief etched on Florence Thompson's face? [iii] Such questions thumb their nose in the face of easy answers. They give birth to even more questions.

The book you are holding demands that we learn to see differently, to weigh possibilities, to question more precisely, to argue for our interpretation, and justify our interpretation cogently and convincingly. Primary sources are means to a higher end—one that applies not only to the social studies, but to every single subject in the curriculum. The book you are holding helps you teach students how to think.

Sam Wineburg

Margaret Jacks Professor of Education and History, Stanford University

[i] Both pictures and captions are reproduced in Aaron Kinney, "Looting" or "Finding"? *Salon*, September 1, 2005, downloaded January 25, 2014, http://www.salon.com/2005/09/02/photo_controversy/

[ii] Arthur Rothstein, cited in James C. Curtis, "Making sense of documentary photography." *History Matters: The U.S. Survey on the Web*, http://historymatters.gmu.edu/mse/photos Downloaded August 24, 2009.

[iii] On the other photos in Lange's series see, James C. Curtis, "Dorothea Lange, Migrant Mother, and the Culture of the Great Depression, Winterthur Portfolio, Vol. 21, No. 1 (Spring, 1986), pp. 1-20. For a strikingly different view of "migrant mother," see the ever-provocative Erroll Morris, *Believing is seeing: Observations on the mysteries of photography*. New York: Penguin, 2011.

Introduction

This Is Not Just a Photograph

Class portrait taken in the 1920s. Austin/Thompson Collection.

Take a look at those faces. Do you see any of your students there? Would they see each other? Or themselves? Think about the kinds of questions you could ask in a second grade class. "Why was this picture taken? Who is the adult standing next to these kids? Is this a picture of one class or a whole school? Are the kids wearing the kind of clothes you wear? What's the same? What's different? Do you think this picture was taken recently?" And what could you ask an eighth grade class? "When do you think this photograph was taken? Do you think you could find out when little girls wore the hairdo that most of these girls are wearing? When did boys wear short pants and long socks? The caption to the photo says that it was taken in the 1920s. In what part of the country did African Americans and whites go to school together in the 1920s?" And then think about the writing assignments that could be based on the photograph. "Choose one of the children in the photograph and write about what you think he or she is like. Give the child you choose a name and an age. Tell about what he or she thinks and feels."

This is a primary source. This class photograph, which was found in an Ohio antique store, is a clue to American history. It is an opportunity to be a detective. It is also what the Common Core State Standards want you to show your kids.

In today's world, educators are being challenged as never before to invite reality into the classroom and allow students to explore it. We are being asked to expose students to the very documents that history is made of, the images that science is based on, the raw material of our lives, and our accumulated knowledge. This is true for a lot of reasons. As we all know, students learn and remember best, not what they are told, but what they discover for themselves. Also, most students learn much better from hands-on problem solving than from simply reading and trying to digest written material. Finally, the Common Core State Standards are making a lot of changes in American education, and one of those changes is a new emphasis on primary source material.

Another emphasis is on the use and interpretation of visual information, whether or not that visual information is a primary source. The modern world demands that students be able to navigate a reality dominated by visual information. Sight is the dominant sense, and modern communications media increasingly appeal to that sense. Educational materials include more and more visual materials with each revised edition. As this material is digitized for use on interactive whiteboards and online courses, as well as apps for tablets, students are being exposed to an abundance of photographs and maps, paintings and political cartoons, charts and graphs.

This means that they need to become visually literate—that is, to develop the ability to look at an image, analyze it, and decode it. And in our opinion, visual literacy is not yet taught particularly well or completely. Students need to "read" images in the same sense that they read text. And often, the same skills are involved. The information and method of analysis in this book can be applied to any type of imagery, primary or secondary. It will help your students approach visual material critically and improve their visual literacy.

As the author/editors of several print documentaries—which are created with visual and text primary sources—we have found that readers and audiences of all kinds respond emotionally and viscerally to imagery and to authentic voices. These evidences of our past evoke a personal reaction—of sympathy, of anger, of compassion—in a way that straight narrative and lists of facts simply cannot. We are not the first to discover this. Ken Burns has made a pretty good career out of doing the same thing on film. His *The Civil War* changed the way most of us look at that terrible conflict, and his other documentaries have been almost as influential. Of course, it's no accident that they're called documentaries. They do not just tell about our history. They document it, with primary sources that most people find fascinating.

> **Photographs and voices—primary sources—touch people in a way that virtually nothing else does.**

Our first book, *The Face of Our Past: Images of Black Women from Colonial America to the Present,* was a documentary treatment of the lives and history of African American women. It landed us on *Oprah.* Her producers based a five-minute segment of the show on the photographs in that book. The photographs spoke so eloquently of the lives of black women that the book soared to the top of the Amazon.com ratings in one day. Photographs and voices—primary sources— touch people in a way that virtually nothing else does.

Our experience with that book and the two that followed it led us to a deep interest in images and primary texts as tools to capture the interest and imagination of students. We began doing presentations in schools, and those presentations have allowed us to see primary sources as remarkable teaching tools and springboards for dynamic and searching discussions. Consider this image from our book *Children of the Depression:*

New Madrid, Missouri, 1938. Sharecropper's son.
Photo by Russell Lee. Library of Congress.

We've shown this photograph to many students, from elementary school to high school, and asked them what they saw. What do you think is the first thing students notice about this photograph? The plow? The hardpan earth? The old-fashioned cap? Almost without exception, students say, "He's really buff. Look at his delts! He's got muscles." Which leads easily into, "How old do you think he is? Do kids of 7 or 8 usually have muscles like that? How do you think a kid that age gets muscles like that? What's he doing in this picture? How hard do you think he has to work? Why do you think a kid that age has to work that hard?"

The students who look at and examine this photograph are finding out about conditions in this child's life in 1938 Missouri for themselves, using the kind of evidence that historians use. Delving into the image brings home the reality of a painful period in American history in a way that the average narrative in a textbook just can't do.

And when you add historical context, even more interesting things happen. Place this photo in the Great Depression. Then ask older students, "Is this what you think of when you hear the words 'Great Depression'?" See where that question leads. Will students contrast this photograph with the images that usually accompany narratives of the historical period—mostly white, adult men standing in breadlines? Could this question lead to a discussion of whether history as we learn it from books is always inclusive or whether sometimes people get left out?

In *Children of the Depression* we also used this text:

> *My dad was shell-shocked in World War I. After they confirmed that, he got a pension and the children got a pension. And I think ours was $80 a month. That was all the cash there was at Grandma's house, where we lived after Mother died. We had some food that was raised there on the farm, but there wasn't much cash. That's what there was for two families and later on three families, when Aunt Emma and her husband and children had to come and live with us.*
>
> *Interview with Frances Tracy, who was a teenager in Western Oklahoma*

This text communicates in a very different, but no less powerful way. Students are likely to feel its emotional content strongly. And they can draw from it a lot of information. "Why did the Tracy children go to live with their grandmother? How did they manage to live on so little money? Why do you think Aunt Emma and her family 'had to' come to live on the farm?"

While the previous examples were historical ones, there are equally useful primary sources for other areas of instruction. For a social studies class on community, for example, you might use this photograph:

Marcela at work in the Green on McLean community garden. Chicago, Illinois, July, 2013. Photograph by Michael Nowak.

This is a snapshot, one of the many kinds of photographs that can be primary sources. It is unposed, and the child in it is not aware of the camera. The caption says that she is working in a community garden. You might ask students to talk about what they see in the photograph *before* you show them the caption. "Where is this girl? What time of year is it? What is she doing? Did she just start working? (Look at her knees!)" Then you could read the caption and ask other questions. "Why would people in Chicago make gardens in their neighborhoods? Why do you think this girl, Marcela, wants to work in the garden?"

Besides our work on visual history books, we've also spent several decades as editors, writers, and image researchers for educational publishers. We know how your textbooks are put together and how the tests you use are written, and we use that knowledge in our discussions in this book. Our approach to primary sources is also informed by a thorough grounding in educational objectives and methods.

The Seven Strategies

Clearly, when students look at these primary sources and are led by their teachers to dig into them, they develop major critical thinking skills. Robin J. Fogarty, Ph.D., one of the authors of *How to Teach Thinking Skills Within Common Core* (2012), has distilled from the Common Core a list of "21 Explicit Thinking Skills that thread across all content areas for student proficiency." Of the 21 thinking skills, a conversation about these sources would ask students to use at least the following: analyzing, evaluating, generating, associating, hypothesizing, clarifying, interpreting, determining, understanding, inferring, explaining, developing, deciding, reasoning, connecting, and generalizing.

It makes sense that a historical investigation would require students to use these skills. In doing the detective work that a primary source requires, they are using their brains in an active and engaged way. They're using the tools of thought that human beings have developed since we first began to develop a sense of the world and time—as hunters, farmers, builders, artists, philosophers, scientists, and historians. They are honing mental skills. And these are skills that readily transfer to written material of all kinds, including author's purpose, determining bias, citing evidence, making inferences, and so on.

In the chapters that follow, we will present a set of seven strategies that you can use to help your students get the most out of a primary source. We've found that these strategies are very effective in teaching with images, and they can be applied just as well to text material. Briefly, here they are:

Strategy 1: Decide what you're looking at.

To begin with, are you looking at a primary source at all? In the early grades, this may be almost the only primary source issue you deal with. Children's and young adult books, even textbooks, are filled with illustrations. Some of those illustrations may be very carefully done to provide as authentic a picture as possible of a particular time period, situation, or person. That does not make them primary sources, and children should gradually learn to recognize this. Children at this age should also learn to distinguish between historical fiction and primary source narratives. This doesn't need to happen in an instant, especially since secondary sources can be useful and appealing ways to introduce students to history. But over time, students should develop an awareness of the nature of a primary source.

At higher levels, this same issue becomes more complex. When you first look at a primary source, you will need to determine, if possible, exactly what it is—what kind of image or text it is, where it came from, and when. For example, a photograph might be a snapshot, a studio portrait, a news photo, a documentary photo, an art photo, or an advertising photo. It might have been made in 1850, 1900, or 2013. How you read each type of image is particular to that type. The same is true for different kinds of written documents. Sometimes identifying the material will be as simple as reading a description, or a caption, in a textbook. Sometimes it can mean beginning with the material as an artifact and determining the information yourself. Sometimes you may need to do research just to know what you're looking at.

Strategy 2:
Determine the purpose and audience.

The purpose of a source is usually integrally connected with its intended audience, so determining the purpose often means beginning with the audience. A studio portrait, for example, is usually intended to be given to friends and relatives. They are its audience. A portrait is usually a collaboration between the photographer and the subject to make the subject look as good as possible for that audience. The people in the portrait you're looking at probably wore their best clothes or clothes that had symbolic value, such as a uniform. They posed, or were posed, to look happy or proud or beautiful. They have a great deal of agency in the creation of the photograph.

In a documentary photo, on the other hand, the photographer is often trying to get the public to pay attention to something unpleasant, wrong, or painful. The purpose of the photograph does not involve showing its subject in the best possible light, and the subject probably has very little agency in the creation of the photograph. He or she might not even know that a photograph is being taken.

As for written material, a diary entry has a very different audience and purpose from a memoir or oral history. The audience for a diary is usually the person who is writing it, and so the writer probably comes as close to telling the truth as he or she ever will. The audience for a memoir is the reading public, and the writer, consciously or unconsciously, probably shapes the narrative in order to get a favorable response from the reader. Clearly, different information can be obtained from a diary than from a memoir.

Strategy 3:
Look for bias.

Looking for bias and understanding how it affects what the text or image communicates is a crucial strategy in viewing a primary source. And bias comes into play on many levels. The personal biases of the author, photographer, or artist are usually reflected in their work. The broader biases of an era or a culture are apparent in almost everything created in and for that era or culture, making it necessary to know some history in order to investigate history.

In both images and text, it is sometimes possible to detect bias from an examination of the source itself. Other times, knowledge of the author and his or her life reveals a bias that would not otherwise be obvious. This strategy helps students develop critical thinking skills that will translate to other areas of their academic lives and helps prepare them to respond to many different kinds of information and influence.

Strategy 4:
Examine closely the source itself.

This is, in many ways, the most interesting part of the whole project. It means really looking at all the details of the material carefully and creatively. If dealing with a primary source is detective work, this is examining the crime scene.

For students in the early grades, this strategy is an excellent exercise for helping to develop visual literacy, whether it is used with a primary or secondary source. When you show students a photograph, for example, and ask them questions that will help them see what's in it, you are helping them think of visuals as sources of information. They are learning to find and interpret clues to the reality being portrayed. For older students, close examination is the aspect of primary source investigation that gives them the strongest feeling of real participation in the discovery and creation of history. It involves keen observation and the ability to bring all their prior knowledge and experience to bear on forming, not opinions, but reasoned judgments about what they're seeing.

While you're doing your detective work—and helping your students do theirs—you'll need to keep in mind what you decided about the purpose of the material and its intended audience. That will affect how you interpret the details you find. And you should form questions that you will probably need to research in order to answer. That's the next strategy.

Strategy 5:
Find more information.

If you're looking at a primary source in a textbook, there may be information in the text that will help you interpret the material. But you and your students may want to know more. And often, there will not be much information to work with. A critical reading of the caption and the understanding that captions are not always accurate is essential. You'll start with what you already know, of course, but then you'll go on to do research. A primary source is an extraordinary launching pad for a research project.

And then you go back to the primary source. Your second, more informed look may reveal details you and your students didn't even notice the first time. It will certainly lead you to different conclusions about some of the things you saw the first time.

Strategy 6:
Consider your own role in the interaction.

This is absolutely crucial. You and your students bring a whole life's worth of experience, cultural conditioning, opinions, and biases to the act of viewing a primary source. If you really want to understand what you're looking at, you need to examine how you're coloring it. Our expectations are very different from those of people living a century ago, for example. Through discussion, students can compare their own viewpoints with those of people in an earlier time and gain great insight into their own assumptions and prejudices.

Strategy 7:
Compare a variety of sources.

Any investigation into history will be more interesting and more accurate if you are able to compare a variety of sources. The more sources, the clearer the picture that emerges.

By looking at a variety of primary sources, students learn to apply the same basic principles of critical thinking in different ways with different kinds of sources. They learn valuable lessons about point of view and bias. And they get experience in synthesizing and integrating information, a skill that will be of great value when the time comes for them to do research papers.

Possibly the most important part of comparing primary sources is that some sources raise questions that other sources may answer. As a result, students are able to actually find historical information to answer their own questions. It's a dynamic, exciting process that can give students a sense of history as a continuing investigation. And the ability to get information about the same situation or event from a photograph, a diary, an interview, and an artifact will allow them to think critically about what they are investigating.

Of course, the process we are laying out here is not a strict linear progression. These strategies provide a framework to a process that is usually a flow rather than a ladder. Analyzing a primary source requires a back and forth between the strategies. "Determining audience and purpose" might be possible only after finding more information. "Examining closely" might occur each time you look at or read the source.

Strategy 3
Bias?

Strategy 5
Find Clarence
Lehr in census?

Other photos of
Clarence Lehr in
Rochester images?

Strategy 6
Boy reminds me
of my cousin.

Don't like the
girls in dresses
on the sidelines.

Strategy 1
News photo,
1921

Strategy 4
Leg brace
Tie?

Clarence Lehr swings a baseball bat as other children watch from behind. Despite the braces on his legs, Lehr hit home runs in this game. Photography by Albert Stone. Printed in Rochester Herald, Mary 15, 1921. Courtesy of Rochester Images, Monroe County Library System.

Strategy 2
Audience:
general public

Purpose: report
on community
events

Strategy 7
Found another
photo. Is it same
Clarence Lehr?

As we go through these strategies in the book, we suggest questions to consider and activities to use with students as well as a few tips and quotations here and there. The examples we use were chosen to make our points as clearly as possible for you, the teacher. Most of them would be appropriate for use with your students, but a few may not be. We trust your judgment.

We also note the particular Common Core State Standards that are met by each strategy and each example. This includes not only critical thinking standards involved in the students' investigations, but also the standards that mandate work with primary sources. Chapter Ten will present more intense activities you can use with your students, and Chapter Eleven will provide advice about and links to websites for finding your own primary sources.

Standards

Common Core, Primary Sources, and Visual Materials

Working with primary sources is specifically mandated by the Common Core State Standards (CCSS). But before we launch into the standards themselves and how we address them, a quick explanation of the coding system follows.

There are three areas of CCSS standards that are addressed in this book: Anchor Standards for Reading (R), Reading: Informational Text standards (RI), and Literacy in History/Social Studies standards (RH). Anchor standards are not divided by grade levels. With the Informational text and Social Studies standards, the grade or grade range follows the RI or RH. In all cases, the number of the standard is last. For example, the Informational Text standard for kindergarteners on asking questions would be CCSS.ELA-Literacy.RI.K.1. If we combined the same standard (#1) for kindergarten through third grade, the standard would read, CCSS.ELA-Literacy.RI.K–3.1.

In the Informational Text standards in fourth grade, students are expected to "compare and contrast a firsthand and secondhand account of the same topic or event" (RI.4.6), implicitly expecting students to have an understanding of primary sources. "Historical, technical, and scientific text," which surely includes primary sources, is called out in grades four and five (RI.4.3, RI.5.3). In sixth grade students are expected to compare and contrast a memoir and a biography (RI.6.9).

Standards focusing on Literacy in History/Social Studies (RH), which start in sixth grade, ask that students analyze primary sources (RH.6–8.1), determine central ideas and summarize primary sources (RH.6–8.2), and compare primary sources with secondary sources on the same topic (RH.6–8.9). The high school social studies CCSS deal with primary sources in even more depth.

Interpretation of visual materials, whether primary or secondary sources, is also specifically called out in the CCSS. Starting in kindergarten, students are expected to begin interpreting the influence of visual materials (RI.K–1.6, RI.K–3.7) in their texts. By fourth grade students are expected to "interpret information presented visually, orally, or quantitatively" (RI.4.7). By middle school the Literacy in History/ Social Studies standards ask students to integrate visual media into print and digital texts (RH.6–8.7) as do the Informational Text standards (RI.6.7). Students are also asked to evaluate and compare and contrast the influence of visual media on how a subject is presented (RI.7–8.7).

These requirements essentially apply to all the content in this book. Therefore we will not call them out specifically—or only rarely. Most of the standards you will see in footnotes in the following pages will be critical thinking standards that are normally applied to text, but which can be taught and taught effectively using both visual and textual primary sources.

National and State Social Studies Standards

In addition to the CCSS, there are national and state standards that your instruction may have to meet. The National Curriculum Standards for Social Studies addresses primary sources in Standard 2: Time, Continuity, and Change. Early grade students are expected to understand that they can learn about the past using, among other things, original sources, such as documents, letters, photographs, and artifacts. They are expected to be able to use photographs and documents to identify continuity and change. Middle grade students are to understand the concept of primary and secondary sources and how to interpret varied sources as well as be able to identify, use, research, and analyze primary sources. Standard 8: Science, Technology, and Society expects early grade students to begin the exploration of different types of media and how that media influences us. Middle school students are expected to understand our dependence on media and technology as well as how cultural context influences media.

Most K–8 state social studies standards include the requirement that students learn to understand and analyze primary sources as well as other visual materials, though the details vary from state to state. For example, in Florida, kindergarten students are expected to have an awareness of primary sources and first grade students an understanding of primary sources. By eighth grade, students should be able to evaluate and compare ideas in primary sources. Additionally, in eighth grade students are expected to be able to analyze maps, photographs, and political cartoons among other types of visual materials.

The Texas Essential Knowledge and Skills (TEKS) expect that kindergarteners will be acquiring information from "a variety of oral and visual sources." By second grade, they are expected to be able to "obtain information about a topic using a variety of valid visual sources," including pictures and artifacts. Also in second grade, they begin interpreting visual material. In third grade, students are to be able to "research information, including historical and current events… using a variety of valid visual resources." Fourth graders should be able to "differentiate between, locate, and use valid primary and secondary sources," including visual materials.

The California state standards say children between kindergarten and fifth grade should be able to differentiate between primary and secondary sources. Students are also expected to be able to "pose relevant questions about events they encounter in historical documents, eyewitness accounts, oral histories, letters, diaries, artifacts, photographs, maps, artworks, and architecture." By sixth through eighth grades, students are expected to "assess the credibility of primary and secondary sources and draw sound conclusions from them."

The Ohio K–8 standards state, "historical thinking includes skills such as locating, researching, analyzing and interpreting primary and secondary sources so that students can begin to understand the relationships among events and draw conclusions." The specific standards begin to include use of primary sources in first grade. Visual primary sources are also mentioned in first grade: "Photographs, letters, artifacts and books can be used to learn about the past." By eighth grade, "primary and secondary sources are used to examine events from multiple perspectives and to present and defend a position."

Conclusion

Whether you are teaching first or eighth graders, this book will provide you with an understanding of how primary and secondary sources are used in our educational materials. It will give you the tools you need to incorporate primary sources in your lessons and to help your students recognize and read them.

Working with primary sources is the best kind of training in critical thinking. Once students have learned to interpret and evaluate primary sources, they can use the same skills when listening to a news show, reading a book or magazine, or, perhaps most important, looking at the Internet. While they're learning about history and the world around them, they will also learn to be thinking, questioning people and citizens.

> Working with primary sources is the best kind of training in critical thinking.

Things to Think About

1. Why is it important to teach primary sources to your students?

2. What aspects of primary source teaching do you think your students would respond to?

3. How could the seven strategies help your students learn needed critical thinking skills?

Chapter One
Primary Sources in History

Sam Wineburg, author of *Historical Thinking and Other Unnatural Acts: Charting the Future of Teaching the Past*, tells this story for TPS Quarterly:

> *When I recently asked Kevin, a sixteen-year-old high school junior, what he needed to do well in history class, he had little doubt: "A good memory."*
>
> *"Anything else?"*
>
> *"Nope. Just memorize facts and stuff, know 'em cold, and when you get the test, give it all back to the teacher."*
>
> *"What about thinking? Does that have anything to do with history?"*
>
> *"Nope. It's all pretty simple. Stuff happened a long time ago. People wrote it down. Others copied it and put it in a book. History!"*

History is not, of course, a memory game. History is a kind of science, but it's a peculiar one, because you can't see what you're studying. You can only see the traces that it has left behind, like the clues at a crime scene. Those traces are what we call primary sources (and to some extent, secondary sources as well, but we'll go into that later). And, clearly, the best way to imbue students with an active, exciting sense of history as a process is to show them the clues—to expose them to primary sources—and possibly even to set them on the path to finding other clues.

In this chapter, we're going to talk about what a historical primary source is. That can sometimes be ambiguous, and it's important that you, the teacher, have a good, clear grasp on it before you start teaching your students. So, before we go into our seven strategies, we're going to try to get rid of the ambiguity.

Simply defined, a primary source is direct evidence of the nature of a time, place, or historical event. It must have been produced by participants in the event, situation, or historical time period being investigated or by witnesses to it. Primary sources are our best clues to what happened in the past or, to put it another way, history. (They are also exceptionally valuable in learning and teaching about the world around us, and we will go into that in the next chapter.)

What Kinds of Things Can Be Primary Sources?

When a crime is committed, the criminal justice system, including law enforcement and the courts, begins an investigation. The goal of that investigation is to determine what happened, in an attempt to bring a criminal to justice. That is probably one of the most common and, to people in today's world, most familiar forms of historical investigation, especially given the popularity of the "cop show." And the clues in that kind of investigation are primary sources. They include these:

Physical Evidence These may be fingerprints or marks left by a crowbar on a window frame or a shred of wool spun and dyed on only one sheep farm in the world and for sale in only one store in New York found in the hinge of the burgled safe. In historical terms, these are sometimes called relics or artifacts and can include almost anything that was created and/or used by a human being during the period under investigation. In textbooks, artifacts are represented by photographs, but you can find historical artifacts in museums, antique stores, and even thrift shops. You and your students have historical artifacts in your homes.

Physical Evidence

Clothing	Furniture	Tools
Cooking utensils	Jewelry	Toys
Dishes	Religious objects	Weapons

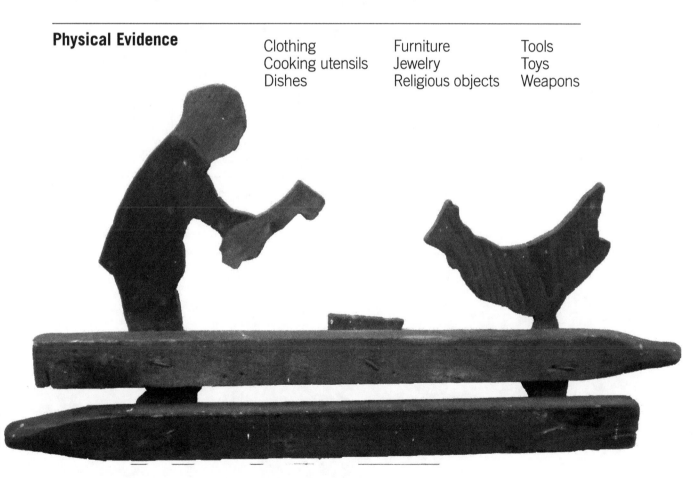

An old wooden toy.
Photograph by Helen Tracy. Austin/Thompson Collection.

Records These include security camera film or tape recordings, but also financial records that prove the suspect was going to lose her house, business, and gold-digging husband if she did not obtain $100,000 by Tuesday. In historical terms, they may include census records or laundry lists or any other kind of record that was created during the period under investigation. (Historians can glean information from the most unlikely sources!) They also include films, audio recordings, and photographs.

Records	Advertisements	Financial accounts	Photographs
	Birth certificates	Military records	Posters
	Census forms	Minutes of meetings	Theatre programs

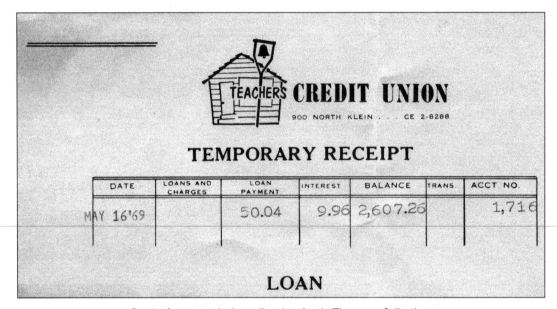

Receipt from a teacher's credit union. Austin/Thompson Collection.

Accounts These are statements by people who participated in or saw a particular event or situation. Sometimes called "eyewitness accounts," these are highly prized in any investigation, whether criminal or historical. They are also viewed with a lot more skepticism than a fingerprint or a birth certificate. Diaries, oral histories, memoirs, and autobiographies are all accounts. They are one person's actual description of the time he or she lived in generally or some event in particular.

Some—but not all—news articles and reports are also primary sources. An article qualifies as a primary source when the person who wrote it actually witnessed the event being described. Conversely, a newspaper article that is not a primary source may include primary source material in the form of reports from people who were witnesses to the event.

Accounts	Affidavits	Journals	Oral histories
	Diaries	Interviews	Police statements
	First-hand reporting	Letters	Speeches

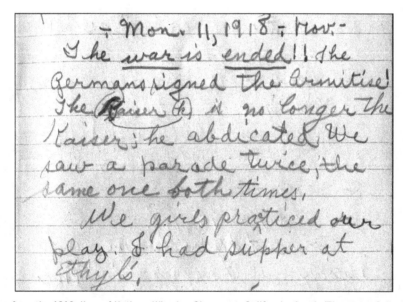

Entry from the 1918 diary of Kathryn Wheeler, Claremont, California. Austin/Thompson Collection.

Now, if you watch cop shows, you know that all of these primary sources are open to interpretation and any of them can be faked. They are clues, and it takes skill to use them to get to facts. Also, one clue may be both physical evidence and a record. The categories are not hard and fast. They're just good ways to think about sources.

Historical sources are particularly valuable when they are supported by other, independent sources. Just as detectives don't build a case on one fingerprint or one interview with a witness, historians don't stop their investigation after reading one diary or looking at one photograph. Two sources are far more valuable than one. In fact, the more sources the better, history-wise.

Sometimes a Primary Source Is Not a Primary Source

It's important to remember that the term "primary source" is just a short way of saying "primary source of information about _____." If you can't fill in that blank, you can't confirm that an item is a primary source. An advertisement about hair lotion from the 1920s could be a primary source if you're looking at ideals of beauty, but it is not a primary source if you're investigating the manufacturing of beauty products in that era. It just doesn't contain that kind of information. A child's diary from California in the 1940s might not be a primary source of information about the war preparations on the West Coast, but it might be a primary source if you're looking at how the war affected the lives of civilians.

Look at this example of a photograph from the Environmental Protection Agency collection at the National Archives.

Miss Junior Texas sitting with friends in her hometown of Leakey, Texas, May 1973.
Photographer, Marc St. Gil, DOCUMERICA Series, National Archives.

This photograph contains a wealth of detail. Students would be able to dig into it for all kinds of information, from the way the young people are dressed to the stumps they are sitting on to the items in the store window. But what is it a primary source of information about? Youth fashion in the 1970s? Beauty pageants in America? The history of youth in America? Economics in small town America in the latter half of the twentieth century?

For a couple of these topics, it's a primary source. For a couple of them, it's not. This is an excellent primary source for youth fashions in the 1970s and for the history of youth in America generally, but it is not a primary source for the economics of small town America or beauty pageants, even if it is a picture of a beauty pageant winner.

The Validity of Primary Sources

Usually, primary sources were created at or very near the time of the event for which they are clues. But that's not always the case when it comes to accounts. Sometimes a person writes about an event that happened many years ago in a memoir, an autobiography, or an oral history. And that brings up an important point. Some primary sources are more reliable than others.

As a general rule, sources that are created closer in time to the event are more reliable than sources that are created later. A soldier's journal entry from the day of a battle may be considered more reliable than a description of the same battle written in a memoir years later.

Sources that are created by people who have no direct interest in persuading the reader or viewer are more reliable than those created by interested parties. We have all heard the varying estimates of the size of a crowd at a political demonstration. The organizers of the demonstration may say that 30,000 people showed up, while opponents of the cause will estimate that there were 3,000 people. A more reliable source than either of these reporters would be an impartial journalist or, better yet, a photograph of the crowd.

And that brings up another point—two independent sources are more than twice as valuable as one. An eyewitness account that is supported by a photograph is more valuable than one without. A photograph that supports something that is written in a diary is more valuable than a photograph alone. If two sources agree with each other, one step has been taken toward establishing a fact. If they don't, the historian has been prevented from accepting as fact what may not be. As the old journalism saying goes, "If your mother tells you she loves you, get a second source."

> **If your mother tells you she loves you, get a second source.**
> **—Popular saying in journalism schools**

Now. Here's one final point. Most of the time, the primary sources you use with your students will not be primary sources at all. They will be what are often called "surrogate primary sources." In other words, they are reproductions of primary sources. This is particularly true of artifacts, which will appear in your text as photographs of artifacts. But it is also true of images and of text, and in the chapters that follow, we will go into the factors you need to be aware of with regard to reproduction. In the meantime, we will continue to refer to surrogate primary sources as primary sources because, for the purposes of the classroom, they provide almost the same information

What Is a Secondary Source?

That brings us to secondary sources. There may be clues in a criminal investigation or in a historical investigation that are very useful even though they are not primary sources. If a barista at a coffee shop overhears a customer say that she burgled a house, that is not admissible in court, but it is of great interest to the detective investigating the case. If a newspaper article reports a fire at a factory, the article is not a primary source for information about the fire unless the reporter was also a witness, but it can be of great interest to a historian investigating the event.

Secondary sources are descriptions or accounts of historical events or situations that are created by people who were not participants or witnesses. They are based on primary sources and can be anything from the newspaper article mentioned above to a history book written 100 years after the event. Usually, as with primary sources, the closer the secondary source is to the event, the more reliable it is. However, it is important to keep the bias of the writer and the time period in mind. Secondary sources about events in Native American or African American history, for example, are often not more reliable when they are closer to the event because of bias at the time.

Secondary sources are created by subjecting primary sources to one or more of the following:

- Analysis
- Interpretation
- Synthesis
- Evaluation
- Generalization

For example, suppose you are the reporter writing the article about the fire. You weren't there, but you interviewed two or three people who were there and who saw at least part of what happened. You looked up information about the building that burned down in the town records. And you have your own opinion about the guy who owned the building because you've run into him back when you were covering the police beat.

So, first you analyze each eyewitness report to get the facts as the witnesses remember them. Then you synthesize those reports, putting together the facts from the different reports. Along the way, you're probably evaluating your sources to decide who is most reliable. And you have to generalize to create a fairly accurate sequence of events. After you add what you've learned about the condition of the building before the fire and evaluate the owner's reputation, you interpret the information. And each one of these processes removes the final story from the raw material of its primary sources.

A hypothetical example could help us see how these processes work in writing history. Suppose you are trying to determine whether the Thomas Johnson who was mayor of the town of Wintergreen was the same person as Tom Johnson, who was a conductor on the Underground Railroad. Perhaps you have the mayor's obituary, which gives quite a lot of information about his life, including when and where he was born and so forth. Then you have a diary entry written by a former slave who was helped by an Underground Railroad conductor somewhere in the vicinity of Wintergreen. The diary includes a good description of the conductor and the house where the escapees were hidden. To find the answer to your question, you would analyze the two sources for specific facts, such as Johnson's age and where his house was located. You would synthesize the two accounts, interpret the information, and so forth. Historians follow this process when they are analyzing primary sources for the real story.

> Secondary sources are what we produce when we do historical work.

In a very real sense, secondary sources are the products of historical investigation. They are what we produce when we do historical work. Now, here's where things might appear to get slippery. Often a source is either primary or secondary, depending on what you're investigating. A newspaper report about a labor strike, for example, might not be a primary source of information about the strike itself. But it could be a primary source if what you're investigating is attitudes about labor during the period in question.

Many of the primary sources you will come across in your educational materials will be these slippery sources. Illustrations from *Harper's* magazine, for example, used in a textbook chapter about Reconstruction, are almost certainly not primary sources of the scenes they are illustrating, even if the textbook includes them in a feature labeled "Using Primary Sources." The creator of the illustration was most likely not at the scene and did not base the artwork on his memory of the event. These types of items might be excellent sources and very valuable, but they are secondary sources. They could only be considered primary sources if one were using them to examine attitudes and perceptions of the era. In other words, they're slippery.

The textbooks and encyclopedias that students usually learn history from are technically called "tertiary sources." When they are written, the authors usually get their information from secondary sources written by historians. However, most of the time, educational publishers and educators don't make this distinction, and these are also called secondary sources. We will not make the distinction in the rest of this book.

Conclusion

History is an active process of investigation, and historical primary sources are its raw materials. They can be used at any grade level and with any group of students. You can differentiate your instruction with these valuable materials through your choice of discussion questions, activities, and approaches, as well as your choice of the sources themselves.

Things to Think About

1. How would the analogy of primary sources to crime clues work with your students?

2. What kinds of primary sources are you already using in your classroom?

3. After reading this chapter, in what way do you view primary sources differently?

Just for Fun

To help students understand what a primary source is, arrange for three or four students to stage a sudden action in the front of the classroom and then exit quickly. Ask volunteers to tell what happened. Ask what the four students were wearing and what each did. Explain that the descriptions, if written or otherwise recorded, would be primary sources.

Chapter Two
Primary Sources and the World Around Us

In history, primary sources are clues to our past. In the natural and social sciences, primary sources are clues to what the world around us is like and how it works. They show your students places most of them will never go and people they will never meet. And in the process, they help your students make personal connections with a very large world.

A kindergarten class in Nam Dimh province, Vietnam. June 1, 2013.
Photograph by Richard Nyberg for the U.S. Agency for International Development.

In the last chapter, we talked about three categories of primary sources: physical evidence, records, and accounts. In social studies in general, these categories apply pretty well. In the earliest grades, photographs are the perfect introduction to primary sources. Even a very young child can look at an image like this one of a group of kindergarten children halfway around the world and respond to simple questions. "Where are these kids? What are they wearing? Do you think it's hot or cold where they live? Are they having a good time? Why do you think so? Do you think they are like you and your friends?"*

As students get older, the photographs and the questions will become more sophisticated and reach into other subject areas. At the same time, text material can be gradually added and students who are already familiar with extracting information and insight from photographs will take to text primary sources much more readily. There are an almost endless number of photographs from hundreds of sources that are available to you to show your students the world. (See Chapter Eleven.) But it's important to keep in mind that many of the photographs in your textbook are not primary sources.

This is the kind of photograph you might see in a social studies textbook. It is a stock photo. That means a photographer took it for the purpose of making money. The textbook publisher would have looked through a lot of photos, chosen this one, and then paid for the right to put it in the book. The same photograph might be used in an advertisement or a brochure. Most stock photos use professional models, and the models are given instructions on what to do and how to behave. This is important to keep in mind, especially since your textbook will not tell you whether the people are models. If this kind of photograph has a caption, it is usually quite general, such as "Families in Malaysia have fun together." We will explain this kind of captioning more deeply in Chapter Three.

*These questions hit reading standards about asking and answering questions, CCSS.ELA-Literacy.RI.2–4.1.

And yet, these photographs can often allow students to develop their visual literacy and use the skills that are necessary for "reading" primary sources. There are some things students can figure out about the photograph of a family in Malaysia just by looking closely and using their prior knowledge. For example, you could start with the most basic question: What does this photograph show and then ask students where they think the photo was taken—in the family's backyard, in a park, in the forest? "What are those things at the left of the picture? Would you usually find a row of benches in a backyard? In a forest? What are the people standing on? Would you find a sidewalk in a backyard or a forest?"*

You can really use primary source images when you teach geography. This topographical map of New Mexico is an excellent example. Although it's reproduced here in black and white, the original satellite photo is in color and very easy for students to "read." It's from the United States Geological Survey, and similar photos are available online for all the states and territories.

Your classroom discussion can focus on identifying topographical features like mountains and lakes. Depending on the abilities of your class, you could compare this primary source satellite photo with a standard map of New Mexico and have students find the names of natural features, such as mountain ranges. You could also work with students to solve the mystery of that large bright spot near the bottom of the image.**

Outside social studies, the categories of primary sources shift somewhat, and the way you use them in class is somewhat different.

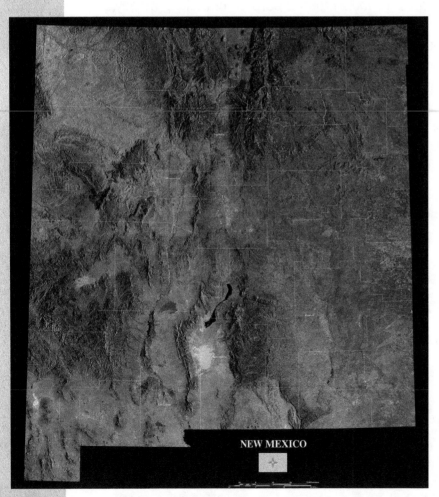

Satellite photo of New Mexico.
United States Geological Survey.

*These questions hit reading standards about asking and answering questions, CCSS.ELA-Literacy.RI.K—3.1 as well as about author's purpose and point of view in CCSS.ELA-Literacy.RI.2.6.

**These questions hit reading standards about asking and answering questions, CCSS.ELA-Literacy.RI.2—3.1.

Primary Sources in Science

In the natural sciences, the whole world falls into the category of physical evidence primary sources. A rare orchid in the Everglades or a weed growing outside the door to your school is physical evidence in botany. A cliff face in the Grand Canyon or a rock on your school playground is physical evidence in geology. The DNA of a long-extinct mammoth is physical evidence in biology, and so are your students. Observing and investigating physical "primary sources" can be a wonderful way for students to exercise their thinking skills, whether they're planting a seed and watching it grow into a sunflower or creating a sundial in the dirt or tracing their own outlines on a large sheet of paper on the floor.

Technically, however, a primary source in the sciences is defined as a record of someone's observation of the natural or human world. This could include a planned experiment by a laboratory scientist, such as a chemist or biologist; weather information, such as written records of daily temperatures and precipitation; and, of course, images.

> **Even when students are far below the reading level needed to read and analyze scientific texts, they can work with visual sources.**

Even when students are far below the reading level needed to read and analyze scientific texts, they can develop skills of observation and analysis working with images and later use those skills with text. And when text and images are combined, the visual sources can reinforce the text in a way that makes it easier to grasp. Images of space, of weather events, of microscopic beings, of animals—all of these are primary sources and have the potential for teaching not only the subject at hand but also critical thinking skills.

Look, for example, at these primary sources, which was once the most numerous bird in the world but was forced into extinction by the early twentieth century. First, we have a photograph of a passenger pigeon on the next page, taken in 1896. In the second or third grade, this picture could be presented with the basic story of the bird's extinction.

"A long time ago, there were more passenger pigeons than any other kind of bird in the world. They flew in huge groups that were sometimes a mile wide and 300 miles long. But there were so many of them that people thought they would always be there. So they killed a lot of passenger pigeons. And about 100 years ago, there weren't any left."

At this level, questions will be simple and very straightforward. "Does this bird look like any bird you know about? What is the background of this photograph? Is the bird free? Is this where it would naturally live?"*

Profile view of a passenger pigeon, a species of pigeon now extinct, with its shadow projected on the wall of the cage behind. Part of a group of pigeons that lived in captivity in the aviary of Professor C.O. Whitman, professor of Zoology at the University of Chicago. Photo by J. G. Hubbard, 1896. Courtesy of the Wisconsin Historical Society.

Next, we have an engraving by John James Audubon. For a fourth, fifth, or sixth grade class, you could show both the photograph and the engraving.

Now, this image is a hand-colored engraving based on Audubon's drawing. Audubon supervised the engraving and the coloring. And Audubon was not only an artist. He was also an ornithologist, trained in observing birds. Not every artist's rendering of a bird would count as a primary source, but Audubon's renderings certainly do. Questions at this grade level can be more sophisticated. Students might be asked to give a detailed physical description of the birds, for example, noting similarities and differences between the two sexes. They could compare the passenger pigeon, as seen in these sources, with the pigeons they are familiar with from parks and sidewalks.

These two images would also be good for discussion of what different information can be learned from each of these sources. "Which of these images do you think is more accurate? What information can you get from the Audubon drawing that you don't get from the photograph? Do you think it would still be useful for people to make drawings like Audubon's now, when taking photographs is so easy?"**

For middle school students, you could add some text to the discussion from Audubon's book *Ornithological Biography*. In autumn of 1813, Audubon was on a trip from his home to the town of Louisville when he saw huge flocks of passenger

*These questions hit reading standards about asking and answering questions, CCSS.ELA-Literacy.RI.2–4.1.

**These questions hit standards about reading closely, CCSS.ELA-Literacy.CCRA.R.1; analyzing multiple accounts, CCSS.ELA-Literacy.RI.5.6; integrating and evaluating content in diverse media, CCSS.ELA-Literacy.CCRA.R.7; and comparing and contrasting two texts, CCSS.ELA-Literacy.CCRA.R.9, CCSS.ELA-Literacy.RI.3–5.9.

Passenger pigeons, male and female. Created by John James Audubon, published in The Birds of America, 1827. (Although the engraving is reproduced in black and white here, it is actually in color, showing the male passenger pigeon to be blue-gray with a reddish breast and the female, which is feeding the male in the painting, to be a duller blue and brown.) Library of Congress.

pigeons flying overheard. Since he had never seen so many of them, he decided to get off his horse, sit on a hill, and count the number of flocks he saw. He took out a pencil and paper and began making a dot for each flock.

> *In a short time finding the task which I had undertaken impracticable, as the birds poured in countless multitudes, I rose, and counting the dots then put down, found that 163 had been made in twenty-one minutes. I travelled on, and still met more the farther I proceeded. The air was literally filled with Pigeons; the light of noon-day was obscured as by an eclipse; the dung fell in spots, not unlike melting flakes of snow; and the continued buzz of wings had a tendency to lull my senses to repose. ...*

> *Before sunset I reached Louisville... The Pigeons were still passing in undiminished numbers, and continued to do so for three days in succession. The people were all in arms. The banks of the Ohio were crowded with men and boys, incessantly shooting at the pilgrims... For a week or more, the population fed on no other flesh than that of Pigeons, and talked of nothing but Pigeons.*

There are a number of other ways primary sources can be used to teach science in the upper grades, but in K–8, artifacts, images, and personal accounts by scientists are among the most effective and accessible.

Primary Sources in Literature

Technically, a primary source in literature is the poem, story, novel, or play itself. That's what an academic would mean when referring to a literary "primary source." But most of the time, educators below college level use the term to refer to an authentic document or image that relates to the work of literature being studied. And it can be very effective to use a primary source from history or science to illuminate a work of literature. For example, if you are teaching John Steinbeck's *Grapes of Wrath*, you might use photographs from the Farm Security Administration, including those of migrating families by Dorothea Lange. If you are teaching John Masefield's *Sea Fever*, you might use photographs that show the extraordinary power and beauty of the ocean, especially if your students have never seen it. If you're teaching Henry Wadsworth Longfellow's "The Village Blacksmith," you might create a visual glossary of artifacts—bellow, sledgehammer, anvil, and forge.

You can also use primary sources to extend the lesson in your reading or literature class into the areas of geography or history. And, of course, primary sources are remarkably effective in sparking creative writing.

Conclusion

Primary sources, both visual and textual, can be used throughout your curriculum to bring your lessons to life. They are not just limited to the upper grades and not just limited to history. You can use primary sources in your science classes by bringing in samples from the natural world or patent drawings of famous inventions. You can use primary source images in social studies lessons about individuals, families, and communities. You can give students in your language arts classes text that will engage their hearts and minds as well as visual stimuli that will augment their reading, extend their imaginations, and spark further creativity. Through all of this your students will be developing crucial critical thinking skills.

Things to Think About

1. How often do you use imagery of all kinds in your classes?

2. How could you include primary sources in your science class?

3. What kind of imagery could you use as a stimulus in teaching writing?

Just for Fun

Work with your students to create a plan for a time capsule. Say, "The material you include will be used by people of another culture or time to understand what your life is like. Include in your plan at least one artifact, one record, and one account."

The Seven Strategies

These are the seven strategies we have developed for looking at and teaching primary sources. It's important to remember that they are not necessarily steps in a sequential process. For any individual primary source, some of the strategies will be far more important than others. One strategy will lead your examination while another will simply add a little insight. In other words, they will flow, not march.

Strategy 1: Decide what you're looking at.

Strategy 2: Determine the purpose and audience.

Strategy 3: Look for bias.

Strategy 4: Examine closely the source itself.

Strategy 5: Find more information.

Strategy 6: Consider your own role in the interaction.

Strategy 7: Compare a variety of sources.

Chapter Three
Strategy 1: Decide What You're Looking at

Strategy 1: Decide what you're looking at.

Strategy 2: Determine the purpose and audience.

Strategy 3: Look for bias.

Strategy 4: Examine closely the source itself.

Strategy 5: Find more information.

Strategy 6: Consider your own role in the interaction.

Strategy 7: Compare a variety of sources.

All right, now you can recognize a primary source. How do you teach your students to do the same? Well, you do it differently with different grade levels.*

Primary Source Recognition in the Early Grades

In the early grades, images and artifacts are the most effective primary sources to use. Textbooks are likely to provide quite a few images, but they will not necessarily be primary sources. Many of them will simply be illustrations and cannot be treated as primary sources.

Your first step with kindergarten and first grade students, then, will be to help them see the difference between a photograph like the one of Marcela in her community garden on page 12 and this image at right.

Since students at the earliest level have not necessarily mastered the difference between real and imagined, this is not an easy thing to do. But it doesn't have to be done all at once.

---

*Discussions and activities in this chapter prepare students to meet standards about reading closely, CCSS. ELA-Literacy.CCRA.R.1; asking and answering questions and citing evidence, CCSS.ELA-RI.1—8.1; integrating and evaluating content in diverse media, CCSS.ELA-Literacy.CCRA.R.7; and evaluating arguments and claims made in a text, CCSS.ELA-Literacy.CCRA.R.8; among others.

Introducing the idea that there is a difference between pictures that are "pretty or fun to look at" and pictures that "show us what the world is really like" is all that's necessary. You can then help students learn to get information from the latter.

You may also want to bring primary sources into the classroom. There's a good chance you already do. When you show students the sweetgrass basket you bought on a trip to South Carolina, you are showing them a primary source artifact. An old postcard you found at a thrift shop, a nut grinder that belonged to your grandmother, a scrap of old handmade lace—these are all historical primary sources. A Mexican chocolate stirrer, a pottery bowl from Indonesia, an olive wood dish from Palestine—these are all primary sources for studying the world around us.

As for primary source images, there are literally millions of them available on the Internet. The important thing is to get your images from websites that identify them properly. A Google search may turn up lots of things that are interesting to look at. But if you get an image from the Library of Congress, the Smithsonian, or any of hundreds of library collections, you will probably know that what you are looking at is a true primary source. You will know where it comes from, when it was created, and what it shows, and you can ask students questions reflecting that. You could also have students compare two sources on the same topic.*

The Next Step in Primary Source Identification

At higher grade levels, the issue of identifying whether an item is a primary source and what kind becomes more complex. The student needs to be able to answer most, or all, of these questions about the material in question:

- Who created the material and why?
- When was it created?
- Where was it created?

Sometimes answering these questions will be as simple as reading a description, or a caption, in a textbook, just as it is for a younger student. However, that is not always the case.

Textual primary sources are usually clearly laid out in educational materials. Teaching your students to recognize block quotes and quotation marks as indicators of primary versus secondary text is usually quite straightforward. The attributions for text primary sources are often clear and easily taught, though not always complete. However, a text will sometimes include a quotation or excerpt with no source other than the name of the author. If you or your students want to find out more about the author and the context of the quotation, it may take some additional library or Internet research.

---

*This discussion hits reading standards about reading closely, CCSS.ELA-Literacy.CCRA.R.1; citing evidence, CCSS.ELA-RI.5–7.1; integrating and evaluating content in diverse media, CCSS.ELA-Literacy.CCRA.R.7; evaluating arguments and claims made in a text, CCSS.ELA-Literacy.CCRA.R.8; and comparing and contrasting two texts, CCSS.ELA-Literacy.CCRA.R.9, CCSS.ELA-Literacy.RI.3–5.9.

Images in educational materials are another story. Until recently, there was not a strong focus on primary sources in history and social studies textbooks. Images in textbooks were usually included as illustrations, to give students some sense of what the world they were reading about looked like. These illustrations were not primary sources, they were not intended to be primary sources, and they were not presented as primary sources.

We are now in a transition stage, during which educational publishers are recognizing the importance of primary sources and are beginning to change their methods with regard to images in textbooks.

There will now be more images in your texts that could be considered primary sources, but they may not be identified in such a way as to make that clear. Even the best educational publishers still usually choose visual elements in their textbooks on the basis of how they look and not whether they will stand up as primary sources. And assuming that any given image is a primary source for the material it has been chosen to illustrate is not always warranted.

You will want to know everything you can about where an image came from and what it's about. Some of that will come from examination of the image itself, and we'll go into that in depth later. But a historical source cannot stand alone. You really have to know its origin. The origin of a piece of writing provides the context and crucial information about the author, which informs how we read a piece of text. The origin helps answer when and why a piece of text was written or an image was created. Consider this piece of text:

> *It's utterly impossible for me to build my life on a foundation of chaos, suffering and death. I see the world being slowly transformed into a wilderness, I hear the approaching thunder that, one day, will destroy us too, I feel the suffering of millions. And yet, when I look up at the sky, I somehow feel that everything will change for the better, that this cruelty too shall end, that peace and tranquility will return once more.*

Just by looking at it what do we know about this piece of writing? Can we even identify whether it is a diary entry, a letter, or an op-ed piece in a newspaper? What if all we knew was that it was written by a teenaged girl? Would that give us much to work with? Now consider the text knowing that this is a diary entry, written on July 15, 1944, by Anne Frank. How does this knowledge change the meaning and significance of the text? Examining how the meaning of the text might change if the author or context were different can be a helpful exercise in the classroom.

Working with imagery can be a powerful introduction for students to the importance of context. Knowing the source of an image is often essential to being able to decode it. One of our favorite examples of this is the following image of a young boy found in the collections at the Library of Congress. While this example might not be appropriate for students in younger grades it could be used for high school and maybe even middle school students.

Looking at the photograph tells us some basic information. It shows an adolescent boy in some kind of workshop. We know it is from an earlier era because of the equipment in the workshop, which is technologically unsophisticated. Looking closely reveals that the boy is working on a shoe. It would not be a wild assumption to think that this image shows a nice, young apprentice to a shoemaker sometime around 1900. But how does our interpretation of the image change when we add the following source information?

Source: Library of Congress

Basic information: Charles Nichols, 16 years old, 1920s,
Colorado reform school.

Does this change what you see in the image? Does the boy look different to you now? What does this information tell you about your own point of view?

A quick e-mail to the Prints and Photographs Division of the Library of Congress revealed the following information: The photograph forms part of the *Ben E. Lindsey Collection.* Lindsey was an early leader in the creation of juvenile court systems in Colorado and California. We were lucky enough to visit the Library to look at the original photograph. That provided even more information. On the back of the photograph, this is written:

> born of criminal parents. His father is in a state prison, serving a life sentence. The boy… once broke jail in Pueblo and ran away from Colorado Springs prison. – His term in the Reform School has just about expired and from what one… warden told me he will eventually be branded as a criminal and find his life ended in prison.

Does the additional information provided by this text change what you see in the image?

This original caption also raises questions of its own. What is fact and what is opinion here? What is the point of view of the person writing the text on the back of the photo? Do you agree with it? Why or why not?

So this one photograph and its original caption information lead down fascinating paths of history and help to hone reading and critical thinking skills.* But how often will a textbook provide you with information like this? Unfortunately, the answer is not very often.

Captions in textbooks frequently don't provide much additional information about the image. When you're working with primary source images from original archives such as the Library of Congress, on the other hand, you're much more likely to find interesting information that adds to—or even challenges—your initial interpretation of it. That's one of the reasons that finding and teaching primary sources from other places is so important.

---

*This kind of photo examination hits standards about close reading, CCSS.ELA-Literacy.CCRA.R.1; asking and answering questions as well as and citing evidence to support analysis, CSS.ELA-Literacy.RI.2–7.1; point of view skills, CCSS.ELA-Literacy.CCRA.R.6, CCSS.ELA-Literacy.RI.3–7.6; and evaluating arguments and claims made in a text, CCSS.ELA-Literacy.CCRA.R.8.

Images in Educational Materials

Knowing something about how the images in your textbooks are found, chosen, and captioned will help you and your students approach these images with a critical eye and determine with some degree of accuracy whether they are primary sources and what their origins are. It will also encourage you to locate primary sources yourself to work on with your students.

There are a variety of types of images in your educational materials. When teaching students to examine and look critically at the images in their educational materials, it is essential that you understand, at least in a general way, where these images originate.

Stock Photos Stock photos are generic photographs, usually using paid models. Many, if not most, of the modern photographs in your textbooks—particularly those showing people—are stock photographs. They are not primary sources. Some examples of stock photo houses are Corbis, Getty, Alamy, Fotolia, and iStock. This is a stock photo:

Stock photograph portraying a student in a contemporary classroom.

Historic Photographs and Other Images Most large educational publishers get their historic photographs and other images—such as engravings and drawings—from vendors, such as Corbis, Getty, or Alamy. These stock photo houses sell photographs created by professional photographers. They also collect public domain images from many different sources. The original versions of the images might be from the Library of Congress or the National Archives or some other public collection. They might also be from news organizations, such as AP, Reuters, or UPI. The stock photo houses sell scans of these images and the license to use them. Publishers use these vendors because they deliver quickly and consistently, they have searchable online databases, and, most important, because these organizations protect the publisher from lawsuits regarding rights and use problems.

Sometimes the image vendor provides the publisher with detailed information about the image and sometimes it doesn't. This is the kind of historic photograph a publisher might get from one of the image vendors:

Employees of the New York Railways Company go out on strike; New York Car Strike has women transported to work in an open-sided male-driven vehicle, created in 1916. Alamy.

The caption below the image includes all the information that the vendor provided to the publisher. It includes the date and the city and the nature of the event, but it does not include any information about who took the photograph and for what purpose. This photograph is a primary source and, although the information is not complete, there is information here for students to delve into. But would the whole caption appear in your textbook? It's not very likely, unless the image was being used in a primary source activity.

Like historic photographs, historic artworks, such as paintings, drawings, and engravings are often gathered from stock houses, such as Corbis or Getty. Many are also retrieved from centralized archives, such as the Bridgeman Art Library, which represents museums all over the world. Some of these images are primary sources, created by people who witnessed an event. Some are not.

This is the kind of historical art that you might see in an American history textbook:

Molly Macauley, known as "Molly Pitcher," loading cannon at the Battle of Monmouth, 1778.

This image is from the Library of Congress. The caption that you see below the image is what you would probably see in a textbook. It does not include who created the image or when it was created. The image has an "old" look to it but, for all we know from the caption, it could have been created by an illustrator for a book published 10, 20, or even 100 years after the event. In fact, according to the LOC caption, the image is an engraving created by J. C. Armytage in 1859 for the book *Battles of America by Sea and Land*, published in 1861. Armytage based the engraving on a painting by Alonzo Chappel, who was born in 1828, 50 years after the event portrayed. (Chappel painted many scenes from the American Revolution, and they show up in textbooks fairly often.) The image was not created by someone who witnessed the event, so it is not a primary source. It is not a good source of information about the actual event. Your students can't discover from it what Molly Pitcher looked like, what she wore, or even what kind of cannon she loaded.

Commissioned Illustrations For the lower grades in particular, many of the images found in educational materials are commissioned illustrations. The publishers describe the picture they want to an artist contracted for the job. Then the artist creates an illustration that meets that description (or spec). Often, illustrators do a great deal of research and create images that are as historically accurate as possible. But they are not primary sources. This image is from *Capstone's Ancient Egypt: Beyond the Pyramids:*

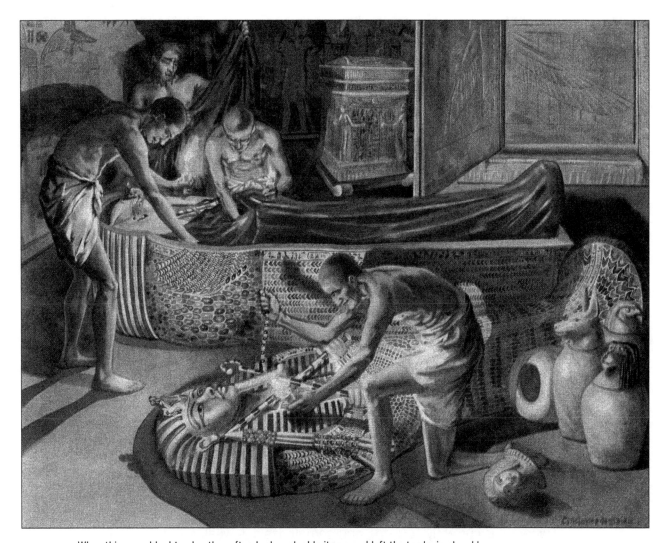

When thieves robbed tombs, they often broke valuable items and left the tombs in shambles.

This is a good illustration. It adds to the book in which it was published by giving students a sense of what a tomb in a pyramid might look like, but it is not a primary source. While we can trust that the artist based elements of the drawing on primary sources, we need to look at it as a secondary source. Therefore, without your help and background knowledge your students should not look to it as a source for details about what an Egyptian tomb and sarcophagus looked like, what was buried with a pharaoh, or who the tomb robbers were and what they wore.

For teachers of ancient history in particular, the materials you use—from your textbooks to Internet websites—will probably include an impressive number of primary sources, principally artifacts but also photographs of archaeological sites. Also included will be modern renderings that show "how cave men lived" or "what the ancient city of Mohenjo Daro looked like." Though it may seem obvious, make sure your students know the difference between the primary sources and these modern renderings and diagrams. It might be useful to use the strategies we will be describing later in the book to analyze the modern illustrations and discuss when the artist might have been basing details on primary source information and when on his or her own imagination, and whether there is any bias involved.

You may have noticed, at this point, just how dependent you and your students are on the captions provided by the publishers of the textbooks you use. And that brings us to the next item when deciding what you are looking at.

Captions in Educational Materials

First and foremost: BEWARE!

This is the information that would be in an ideal caption:
- What is the subject of the image?
- When was the image created?
- Where was the image created?
- Who created it?
- In what was it originally published?

Unfortunately, many captions are generic and give the viewer very little—or no—specific information that adds information to the "reading" of an image. And even if a caption writer wants to use information about a historic image in a given caption, the writer will turn to the vendors from whom they get their images. As we noted above, the information from these vendors is often incomplete. And it might not always be terribly reliable. Sometimes the information is detailed and accurate (most images from the Bridgeman Art Library, for example, include specific information about where an image came from, when it was created, who created it, and where it is currently housed), and sometimes it is weak and uninformative.

This is the information from the Library of Congress for a photograph by Frances Benjamin Johnston.

Title: [Students in a chemistry class conducting an experiment, Western High School, Washington, D.C.]

Creator(s): Johnston, Frances Benjamin, 1864-1952, photographer

Date Created/Published: [1899?]

Medium: 1 photographic print: cyanotype.

Reproduction Number: LC-USZ62-50356 (b&w film copy neg.)

Rights Advisory: No known restrictions on publication.

Call Number: LOT 2749, no. 005 [item] [P&P]

Repository: Library of Congress Prints and Photographs Division Washington, D.C. 20540 USA

This is a good caption, generated from this information:

Students in a chemistry class conducting an experiment, Western High School, Washington, D.C., about 1899. Photography by Frances Benjamin Johnston. Courtesy of the Library of Congress.

But this is what you are just as likely to see in a textbook:

Students in the 1890s worked hard in their science classes.

Clearly, captions for stock photos and commissioned illustrations will be about moving forward the ideas in the text and won't refer to the origins of the image. None of us expects an illustration of Little Bear and Duck reading a treasure map in a third grade social studies reader to say "Illustration commissioned by Publisher X and created by Artist Y in year Z." However, we often believe that if we see a historic photo or illustration, the information in the caption will accurately tell us more about that specific image. That is the implication of a caption and of the educational standards related to reading text features, such as captions.*

Unless the lesson is very specifically about visual literacy (and sometimes even if it is), captions for primary sources are also usually used solely to move forward the educational content of the textual material. In a lesson that touches on coal mining, a photograph of a group of miners might have the caption, "Men worked long hours in the mines." No reference might be made to the source of the photograph, who took it, why, when, and where. And it is not unknown for captions to be inaccurate or misleading. For example, that mine photograph might include several children among the workers who are referred to in the caption as men.

---

*This is explicitly noted in the standard about using text features, such as captions, CCSS.ELA-Literacy.RI.3.5 and implicitly in standards about integrating visual information with other information in print and digital texts, CSS.ELA-Literacy.RH.6–8.7.

In the process of creating educational materials, imagery is often researched by people who did not write the text. In most cases, the image researchers find and the publishers use photographs that depict the specific situation. But, in a pinch, an image may be used that is seen as an acceptable substitute. For example, a photo researcher might be asked to find a photograph of gold mining in West Africa for a geography textbook. However, the researcher is only able to find (using the sources noted above) a picture of gold mining in South Africa. From the perspective of the writer, designer, and publisher, the photograph is evocative and it shows what gold mining in West Africa looks like, even though it was taken in South Africa. The caption written by the lesson writer, possibly before the photo was even chosen, is something generic, such as, "Gold is an important natural resource to West African economies." This might be fine as an illustration and the caption isn't technically inaccurate, but it breaks the rules of primary sources. Happily this might be changing somewhat. With the growing importance of visual literacy and use of primary sources in the classroom, more attention is being paid to captions in educational materials.

> With the growing importance of visual literacy and use of primary sources in the classroom, more attention is being paid to captions in educational materials.

Obviously, then, you need to teach your students to read captions critically. Help your students understand that they need to ask and answer questions about the caption as well as the image.*

- What is the main purpose of this caption? Is it a direct statement about the image or is it a general statement about the content of the lesson?
- Does this caption add to my knowledge of what the image is showing or how I see/interpret this image?
- Does the caption give information about the source of the image?
- Does the caption accurately reflect what is in the photograph?

Students are expected by the Common Core State Standards to use text features, such as captions, to help them understand a text. When appropriate, students should also be helped to read those captions critically. To meet this standard with captions, you probably need to look beyond your textbook for primary sources for your students.

Conclusion

Whether you're looking at material in your textbook or bringing primary sources into the classroom yourself, the first thing you need to do is make sure you know what you're looking at. This is the foundation for all of the other work to come.

---

*These questions hit the reading standard about using text features, such as captions, CCSS.ELA-Literacy.RI.3.5.

Things to Think About

1. How has this chapter changed the way you look at materials in your textbook?

2. Review the images and captions in one chapter of your social studies or American history textbook. How complete are the captions?

Just for Fun

Have students bring photographs from home and write captions for them. Ask them to share their captions with the class and talk about how complete they are.

Chapter Four
Strategy 2: Determine the Purpose and Audience

Strategy 1: Decide what you're looking at.

Strategy 2: Determine the purpose and audience.

Strategy 3: Look for bias.

Strategy 4: Examine closely the source itself.

Strategy 5: Find more information.

Strategy 6: Consider your own role in the interaction.

Strategy 7: Compare a variety of sources.

In the last chapter, we explored Strategy 1: Decide what you're looking at. We looked at how you can identify a text, artifact, or image as a primary source. We looked as well at how you and your students can determine what the material is and—if at all possible—how it came to exist.

Strategy 2 begins the process of interpretation. "Determine the audience and purpose of the primary source." This involves asking a number of questions.

- Who was the intended audience? Who did the person who created the text or image expect would see it?
- Why was the material created?
- If there is a human subject—as in an image or an interview—what was that person's participation?

All of these elements will influence your interpretation of the text or the image.*

---

*Discussions and activities in this chapter prepare students to meet standards about close reading, CCSS. ELA-Literacy.CCRA.R.1; asking and answering questions as well as citing evidence, CCSS.ELA-Literacy.RI.K—8.1; using text features, such as captions, CCSS.ELA-Literacy.RI.1—3.5; and determining an author's purpose, CCSS. ELA-Literacy.RI.K—8.6; among others.

Audience and Purpose

Determining a primary source's purpose begins with figuring out the intended audience. One of the most important questions is whether the text or image was created to be public or private.

For the younger grades, you will probably need to identify the type of material for the students before you begin asking questions. "This is a diary entry. Did the person who wrote it mean for other people to read it? This is a picture from a newspaper. Did the person who took it mean for other people to see it? This is from a letter. Did the person who wrote it mean for other people to read it? This is a family snapshot. Who would probably look at it?"

Often, you can go more deeply into the question of audience and purpose. But again, you and the students need to identify the type of document or image you're looking at and its purpose. Sometimes, this is very simple.

> *July 28 –*
>
> *Went up to Uncles get some*
>
> *butter ... I have been sick with the*
>
> *belly-ache ... Very warm.*
>
> *Diary of Sarah Gillespie*

Clearly, this is a diary entry, and the audience for a diary entry is usually only the writer. Its purpose might be to simply record the day's events or it might be to process deeply private feelings and emotions. (As Anne Frank wrote, "When I write, I can shake off all my cares.") It is usually safe to assume that a diary is basically truthful about what it reports, even though it may be limited to the diary writer's personal experience and point of view.

In other cases, students will need to look for clues to the type of document they are looking at and its purpose. These are some of the questions you might ask to help them:

- Does the caption tell you what kind of text you're looking at and why it was written?
- Are there any other text features that help you?
- Does the language of the text give you a clue?
- Are there clues in the content?

Look at the following text example:

> *My name among my own people was "Ah-nen-la-de-ni," which in English means "Turning crowd" or "Turns the crowd," but my family had had the name "La France" bestowed on them by the French some generations before my birth, and at the institution my Indian name was discarded, and I was informed that I was henceforth to be known as Daniel La France.*

It made me feel as if I had lost myself. I had been proud of myself and my possibilities as "Turns the crowd," for in spite of their civilized surroundings the Indians of our reservation in my time still looked back to the old warlike days when the Mohawks were great people, but Daniel La France was to me a stranger and a nobody with no possibilities. It seemed as if my prospect of a chiefship had vanished. I was very homesick for a long time.

From *An Indian Boy's Story,* by Ah-nen-la-de-ni

The caption we put on the text here shows how it would ordinarily be identified in a textbook. The caption tells you that it was written by Ah-nen-la-de-ni and is about an "Indian Boy." Because it has a title, it was probably written for publication. The use of the first person indicates that the story is about the writer, Ah-nen-la-de-ni, himself. The writing doesn't sound like someone just talking, and that's a clue that this is not an oral history or interview. It is probably a memoir. In fact, it is just that, and it was published in *The Life Stories of Undistinguished Americans as Told by Themselves,* edited by Hamilton Holt in 1906. Its audience was the public, and its purpose was to inform people about the life of a young Native American boy in the last decades of the nineteenth century.*

Degrees of privacy and differences in audience are good clues to interpretation of primary sources. However, some students may have difficulty with them. Today, with Twitter, Tumblr, and Facebook, many people put on the Internet what they would in the past have kept to themselves and their families. Helping students understand that people once wrote deeply with an expectation of privacy is essential in interpreting primary sources.

For older students, primary source texts are an excellent avenue to explore issues of privacy so important today. You could use some of the following questions to spark discussion.

- How would a person write differently if he or she did not expect anyone else to read the document?

- What differences might there be between how someone would write to a trusted friend versus an adversary with whom he or she had to work?

- What about works where the audience was the public at large and the expectation was that anyone anytime could read what was written?

Images are a very effective way to introduce your students to the task of determining the audience and purpose of a primary source. Just as with text, there are various categories of visual primary sources, and each also has an intended audience. We're going to do a breakdown of the types of visual material that can be primary sources and that you'll often see in textbooks.

*This kind of analysis meets standards about close reading, CCSS.ELA-Literacy.CCRA.R.1; asking and answering questions as well as citing evidence, CCSS.ELA-Literacy.RI.K–8.1; and determining an author's purpose, CCSS. ELA-Literacy.RI.K–8.6.

Drawings and Paintings In the era of photography, it's easy to forget that people once depended on the skills of artists to show them the world they could not see themselves. Teams of explorers took artists with them to draw hitherto unknown sites. Artists went on journeys to other lands and drew images to sell in their own countries.

Until well into the nineteenth century, artists were also the equivalent of National Geographic photographers and photojournalists. And they were the recorders of scientific investigations. Illustrations of plant and animal species, for example, were carried out with extraordinary care and skill. (See the Audubon illustration of passenger pigeons on page 37, for example.)

Even during the twentieth century, artists often were the recorders of life when photography would have been cumbersome or impossible. The artist Ivan Albright was a medical illustrator in a hospital in France during World War I, at a time when access to photographic equipment, supplies, and a darkroom would have been extremely difficult. Before photography, artists also drew or painted the portraits of famous people and offered them for sale. The work of all these eyewitness artists is primary source material, with a variety of original audiences, all of which need to be taken into consideration.

Formal Portraits Formal portraits were among the earliest photographs, and they are still created today. They are usually taken in a studio by a professional photographer. Older studio photographs often have special backdrops painted with different kinds of scenes. These backdrops created the illusion that the subject was sitting in a beautiful garden, in a fancy room, or in front of a window. Later backgrounds became blank, monochromatic sheets.

As with the snapshots we're all familiar with, the audience for most studio photographs was friends and family. More than with snapshots, however, there is a sense with formal portraits that they are being made for posterity, to link with the ensuing generations. In the early years of photography (and into the 1930s and 1940s for poorer people), a formal studio portrait might be the only time a person's likeness was created. This means that studio portraits were serious events.

Another reason that many people in formal portraits from the nineteenth century look so serious is that exposure times were slow, so subjects had to sit completely still for quite a long time. The earliest photographic process, the daguerreotype, required that the subject sit perfectly still for up to a half an hour. Needless to say, the process was often unsuccessful. Later, the exposure time was reduced to under a minute. This was much better, but still must have seemed endless. (Time yourself and try smiling naturally for 45 seconds.)

I Sell the Shadow to Support the Substance.

SOJOURNER TRUTH.

Carte-de-visite portrait of Sojourner Truth that she sold to support herself and her crusade for justice. Library of Congress.

Just as with painted portraits, studio photographs of the famous were made for public view and some were even sold to raise money for their subjects. The statement on this carte-de-visite portrait of Sojourner Truth, for example, expresses this baldly: "I sell the Shadow [the photograph] to Support the Substance [Truth herself]."

In addition to studio portraits, other kinds of formal portraits include class photographs, photographs of sports teams, and club or company photographs.

News Photo News photographs are taken to show people what is happening in their world. News photographers consider their work journalism, and they sometimes take great risks to "get the shot." Obviously, their audience is the public at large, and they sometimes have a huge impact on public opinions about current events. This type of photograph is often used in history books and textbooks because they give students a sense of what events actually looked like.

Documentary Photo Documentary photographs are similar in many ways to news photographs, but the people and events in them are not usually part of the daily news. Documentary photographers take pictures of things that interest them, things that they care about, and often, things they believe should be changed. Documentary photographers quite often have an overt agenda. The purpose of many documentary photographs is not only to inform, but also to convince. As with news photographs, the audience might be the general public, but it might also be a specific group of decision-makers.

Snapshots Snapshots are a kind of photograph that most of us have taken and been pictured in. They are usually taken by people who are not professional photographers, although they might be very good at taking pictures. They are generally informal, showing friends and family living their lives, often at special events like birthday parties or on a vacation. Before the 1960s, most snapshots were black and white. Since then most snapshots have been in color. When examining a pre-digital-era snapshot as a primary source, it is important to keep in mind that the only captions on most snapshots, if they exist at all, are a few words scrawled on the back of the photograph. On many snapshots, though, the month and year they were taken are recorded on the side.

The audience for snapshots in the past was usually friends and family and there was no expectation that the images would be seen by—or even be of interest to—a broader public. Today, with the advent of the social network on the Internet, that has changed.

> To show your students examples of all of these different types of images, you can go online to our website, www.onehistory.org.

Art Photo Art photographs are also for the public at large but their purpose is usually to show us something beautiful or interesting. Edward Steichen, for example, was an important art photographer. Art photographs may help us look at the world in a new way, but they are not usually used as primary source material because of the degree to which art photographers manipulate their subject matter. However, Edward Steichen's photographs of Georgia O'Keefe, while works of photographic art, also show us what that great painter looked like. And Ansel Adams photographs of Yosemite National Park serve as historical and scientific documents as well as remarkable works of art. Of course, other photographs, especially documentary photographs, often have great artistic value, even if that was not the photographer's primary purpose in taking the picture.

There are a few kinds of material that are fundamentally visual but with text, such as the images listed on the next page. They are often used in textbooks, in part because they meet the standards for analyzing and interpreting visual material, and they do not require special training in visual literacy on the part of the writers of the educational material. These can be valuable sources.

Art photo by Helen Tracy, 2011. Austin/Thompson collection.

Advertising Images Advertising photographs and drawings are different from most of the other images we've discussed. They are posed, usually with actors, to sell a product. The audience for these images is the purchasing public, especially children and young adults. The purpose of an advertisement is to convince the viewer that the product will make the viewer happy, pretty, sexy, or strong. Sometimes the photograph features a celebrity. The suggestion is that the person in the photograph is famous because he or she uses the product or that the product is trustworthy or worthwhile because the celebrity uses it.

Political Cartoons Political cartoons are a very special kind of art. Their purpose is very clearly to influence the opinions of the public, and they use some very powerful verbal and visual techniques—such as symbolism and physical stereotyping—to do so. They are often deceptively simple and can be difficult for people of a different era to interpret. They reveal a great deal about the attitudes and culture of the period in which they were created.

Maps Textbooks use maps of all kinds, and some of them are primary sources. If a navigator, an explorer, or a surveyor created a map, it may be a primary source with regard to the actual layout of a part of the world. That's rare because most of the maps we see were not made by the explorers themselves. On the other hand, if a map was created by a cartographer from information given to him by explorers and other travelers, it may be a primary source for information about what people at that time and in that place thought the world was like.

Here's an example of a photograph that you and your students could identify.

Bing Miller, of the Philadelphia Athletics, is tagged out at home plate by Washington Nationals catcher "Muddy" Ruel. National Photo Company, 1925, Library of Congress.

- What kind of photograph is this?
- Why do you think that?
- Who was the intended audience for this photograph?
- What was the purpose of the photograph?

Possible answers: It's a news photograph. It is a photograph of an event that would have been reported in a newspaper. Its intended audience was people who read the sports pages of a newspaper. Its purpose is to show what happened in a baseball game between the Philadelphia Athletics and the Washington Nationals.*

Agency

Images of people are different from most text primary sources (with a few exceptions, such as interviews and oral histories) in that there are two people with some control over the creation of the material. As defined by Merriam-Webster's dictionary, agency is "the capacity, condition, or state of acting or of exerting power." In photography, agency is used to refer to the way in which, and the degree to which, the subject of a photograph has control over how he or she is portrayed. The agency of the subject is therefore part of the point of view of the image.

Agency is a key element in examining and interpreting visual primary sources that picture human beings. You can begin the discussion of agency with your students by examining self-portraits. Students will probably be most familiar with self-portraits through "selfies," photographs a person takes with his or her cell phone and then sends to friends or posts on a social network. Artists also make self-portraits, some of the most famous having been done by Rembrandt and Van Gogh. Photographer Cindy Sherman has also used herself as the subject of many of her works. Self-portraits—like autobiographies and diaries—provide the greatest agency for a subject because the subject and the author are one and the same. The author has total control over how he or she is shown and even, whether the image survives.

> An interesting activity (if approached with care) might be to have students create self-portraits (either through photographs or drawings) of themselves and then to create a portrait of a friend.

The subject also has considerable control over a studio portrait. A studio portrait is usually a collaboration between the photographer and the subject because the subject chooses to have a portrait made. Most people want to look nice for the camera, so they put on their best clothes. They want to tell the story that they are happy, healthy, and proud. In older, formal portraits people sometimes wanted to record what they did for a living, so they wore their work clothes or uniforms.

---

*This analysis meets standards about reading closely, CCSS.ELA-Literacy.CCRA.R.1; asking and answering questions as well as citing evidence, CCSS.ELA-Literacy.RI.K–8.1; analyzing text features, CCSS.ELA-Literacy. RI.3.5; and determining an author's purpose, CCSS.ELA-Literacy.RI.K–8.6 and how that purpose shapes content, CCSS.ELA-Literacy.CCRA.R.6.

Of course, studio portraits of children don't quite fit this model. Children seldom have any say about whether they will be photographed. They are usually dressed by their parents and posed by either their parents or the photographer.

In other formal portraits, such as class photos or company photos, the subject has very little control over anything but the expression on his or her face. That's one of the reasons that a lot of class photos feature at least one grimace, one pair of deliberately crossed eyes, or one duckface.

Comparing studio portraits with news/documentary photographs is an excellent way to examine agency in imagery. In news and documentary photos, people might not even know they are having their picture taken. They might not have been asked if they want their picture taken. The main point is that the agency of the subject in a news or documentary photo is much less clear.

Photograph purchased on eBay. From the Austin/
Thompson collection. Judging from the physical
photograph type and internal evidence,
it was taken in the 1920s.

Consider the two photographs on these pages.

In discussing these images with your students, you could ask these questions:

- Did the subject know the picture was being taken?
- Did the subject choose to have the picture taken?
- Did the subject have control over the clothes he or she is wearing in the picture?
- Did the subject choose the setting for the photograph?
- Did the subject pose for the photograph?

The teenaged girl in the picture at left, which we purchased on eBay, clearly knows that her picture is being taken. She has almost certainly arranged for it to be taken and is paying the photographer. She has dressed herself in very nice clothing. (When we were in the decision-making stage for our book *America's Children,* we gave this photograph and the girl in it the name "Classy.") She may have chosen the painted backdrop the photographer used, or at least agreed to it, and the chair as well. The photographer may have suggested the pose, or she may have simply taken it, but it is clearly a pose she is comfortable with. She has a lot of agency in this photograph.

The teenaged boy in the bottom picture did not seek out a photographer to take his picture. It was taken by the documentary photographer John Vachon for the Farm Security Administration. He did not dress up for the photograph, and the setting is the place where the photographer found him. Whether he knew he was being photographed, we do not know. It's possible that he took this pose for the photographer, but it's likely the photographer saw him in this pose and snapped the shot. Whether he had any agency in the creation of the photograph is doubtful.*

Examining this photograph or one like it with your class can be an opportunity to extend the discussion of privacy introduced earlier. If a person does not know his or her photo is being taken, is that an invasion of privacy? How much power does that person have in the situation?

Washington, D.C., August 1938. Unemployed youth. Photographed by John Vachon for the Farm Security Administration. Library of Congress.

*This analysis meets standards about reading closely, CCSS.ELA-Literacy.CCRA.R.1; asking and answering questions as well as citing evidence, CCSS.ELA-Literacy.RI.K–8.1; analyzing text features, CCSS.ELA-Literacy. RI.3.5; determining an author's purpose, CCSS.ELA-Literacy.RI.K–8.6, and how that purpose shapes content, CCSS.ELA-Literacy.CCRA.R.6.

Many of these questions involve conjecture. The point is not to come to an absolute and factual conclusion, but to look at details of the photograph to determine—as much as possible—the relationship between the photographer and the subject.

Snapshots are another type of photograph where the examination of agency can be a fascinating and illuminating exploration. Snapshots are usually trying to tell the story of a happy family. Older snapshots were often taken by an adult to record happy important family events, such as birthdays, graduations, and holidays. More recently, children and adults take snapshots, often with their cell phones.

When discussing or interpreting snapshots with your students, you could ask some of these questions.

- Who takes most of your family snapshots?
- In the snapshots your family has from the past, what are people doing?
- Have you ever been told to smile for the camera?
- Do you think everyone in a snapshot is as happy as they look in the moment the photograph was taken?

Consider this family snapshot:

Photograph purchased on eBay. Judging from the photograph type and internal evidence, it was taken in the 1960s or 1970s. Austin/Thompson Collection.

- What kind of image is this?
- Why do you think that?
- Who was the intended audience for the photograph?
- What was the purpose of the photograph?

Now add agency:

- Did the subjects in this photograph know the picture was being taken?
- Did the subjects in the photograph pose for their picture?
- Did they want their picture taken?
- Did they have control over how they were portrayed?
- What evidence from the photograph can you provide to support your conclusions?

In a class discussion, these are the kinds of answers that students might have to the questions above: It's a snapshot. It can be determined to be a snapshot because it's casual, taken outdoors, seems to be from the 1960s or 1970s when snapshots were common, is not showing a social crisis or injustice, and is not about a news event. Its intended audience was probably friends and family, and its purpose was to be a remembrance of a happy holiday and a record for the family of the subjects when they were children.

The kids knew the picture was being taken. The boy posed. The girl either posed but wasn't happy about having her picture taken or didn't pose or was caught before she set up her pose. The boy is looking at/aware of the camera. His body is open and in a confident pose. The girl is not looking directly at the camera. Her shoulders are hunched. Her lips are pursed. She is looking down. Based on their expressions, the boy wanted his picture taken and the girl probably did not. The only control they had was in how they posed and possibly how the toys are set up. The way they dressed wasn't based on having their picture taken.

These answers are just possible conclusions that can be drawn about this image. There are other ways to interpret it. It is in the exercise of thinking about audience and agency that the lessons are learned and critical thinking skills applied. In addition to being key to interpreting an image, critically examining photographs for the agency of the subject can introduce students to concepts of perspective (point of view), power, and historical context.*

The question of what type of photograph an image is and what its audience and purpose are is often straightforward. However the question of whether the subject of a photograph has agency can be simple or it can be an extended class discussion that is part of a deep analysis. It all depends on the photograph, the subject, and the age of the students. In the chapters that follow, we will describe in detail how to conduct a deep and detailed analysis of an image.

---

*This analysis meets standards about reading closely, CCSS.ELA-Literacy.CCRA.R.1; asking and answering questions as well as citing evidence, CCSS.ELA-Literacy.RI.K–8.1; analyzing text features, CCSS.ELA-Literacy. RI.3.5; determining an author's purpose, CCSS.ELA-Literacy.RI.K–8.6, and how that purpose shapes content, CCSS.ELA-Literacy.CCRA.R.6; and interpreting visual information, CCSS.ELA-Literacy.RI.4.7.

Conclusion

Knowing the purpose of a primary source and the audience for which it was intended is a crucial step in reading and understanding the material. Determining the purpose and audience also engages key critical thinking skills. No real analysis of a primary source is possible without this strategy.

Things to Think About

1. How important do you think the audience is in determining the purpose of a primary source?

2. What are the most common types of images in your textbooks?

3. Do your students have a strong sense of what is public and what is private? Why or why not?

Cogent Quotation
A photograph is a most important document, and there is nothing more damning to go down to posterity than a silly, foolish smile caught and fixed forever.

—Mark Twain

Chapter Five
Strategy 3: Look for Bias

Strategy 1: Decide what you're looking at.

Strategy 2: Determine the purpose and audience.

Strategy 3: Look for bias.

Strategy 4: Examine closely the source itself.

Strategy 5: Find more information.

Strategy 6: Consider your own role in the interaction.

Strategy 7: Compare a variety of sources.

Now that we have determined (as much as possible) the origin of a primary source and its intended audience and purpose, we can begin to look at any possible bias in the material. Like determining audience and purpose, recognizing bias in a textual or visual primary source is essential to being able to interpret and understand it.*

Bias as defined by the Oxford English Dictionary is "an inclination, leaning, tendency, bent; a preponderating disposition or propensity; predisposition *towards*; predilection; prejudice." Almost any primary source you use will show some form of bias, with the exception of artifacts and certain kinds of records. There is unlikely to be any detectable bias in a laundry list or a surveyor's map, for example. But even a census record can have bias. Until 1960, for example, the race of the people in the household was decided by the census taker, and a family might show up as "mulatto"—a term used on the census until 1930—in one census, black in another, and white in still another.

Bias can be mild or extreme. It can influence slightly or totally distort. You'll need to remind your students that having a bias does not necessarily make a primary source unreliable, but understanding a source's bias is essential to interpreting it.

Sometimes bias is clear at a glance, as it usually is in political cartoons. The next page shows two different political cartoons featuring Abraham Lincoln. They have different biases towards Lincoln.

---

*Discussions and activities in this chapter prepare students to meet standards about asking and answering questions as well as citing evidence, CCSS.ELA-Literacy.RI.K–8.1; explaining events and ideas in a historical text, CCSS.ELA-Literacy.RI.4–6.3; determining an author's purpose and bias, CCSS.ELA-Literacy.RI.4–8.6; drawing on information from multiple sources, CCSS.ELA-Literacy.RI.4–6.7; and comparing and contrasting two texts on the same topic, CCSS.ELA-Literacy.RI.3–8.9.

"The sportsman upset by the recoil of his own gun." Cartoon by. Jo. Miller, 1864. Speech balloon reads: "Begorra, if ye wor at the end o' th' gun, ye wouldn't flap yer wings that way, ye villin!" Library of Congress.

In this cartoon, President Lincoln is shown as a silly man who has been scared by his own gun. Even without knowing the political situation the cartoon refers to—and the fact that there was great prejudice against the Irish at the time—students can clearly see the bias against Lincoln. The next cartoon shows something different.

Cartoon by Joseph E. Baker, 1865. The speech balloons say: "Take it quietly UNCLE ABE and I will draw it closer than ever!!" "A few more stitches ANDY and the good old UNION will be mended!" Library of Congress.

Here, the cartoonist has portrayed President Lincoln as a tired but kindly man who is working to repair the Union after the Civil War. It shows a much more positive bias on the part of the cartoonist towards Lincoln. Again, the visual representation is obvious apart from the words. Bias expressed visually is extremely common in political cartoons. In fact, it's pretty much the cartoonist's stock in trade.

In a primary source text, the author's bias may be detectable in his or her language. Read, for example, this excerpt from the book *Abraham Lincoln,* by M. W. Delahay, first published in 1870 in Leavenworth, Kansas.

> *But few men have ever existed, whose lives have been more marked by the predominance of those humble and ostentatious virtues, which are so inseparable from our ideas and impressions of the martyred President; and since the day of the Calvary and the Cross, perhaps no man will be found to have stamped upon the future a more enduring record, or marked a grander epoch in the history of the world, than that accomplished by the simple mind, and pure heart of the murdered Lincoln.*

It seems clear from just this one paragraph that Mr. Delahay had a strong bias in favor of President Lincoln, a bias that might easily be described as hero worship. Delahay's word choices alone are enough to reveal his strong feelings. Another way to determine the bias of a creator of material is to know something about both the creator and the material's context. This would be revealing in the case of Delahay, since he was a friend of the president's, a fervent supporter of Lincoln's political party, and a Lincoln appointee to a federal judgeship. He also wrote the book only a few years after Lincoln's death, when many people in the United States and around the world saw Abraham Lincoln in the glow of martyrdom. Nonetheless, this book may have valuable information in it simply because Delahay was close to Lincoln. It is just important to read it critically and with an awareness of its bias.

Bias in Photographs

The word *stereotype* doesn't actually come from the stereographic photos of the nineteenth century, but it might as well. The stereoscope was a device that allowed the viewer to look at pictures in a primitive but effective form of 3-D, and it was very popular from the 1860s until well into the twentieth century. Several firms, such as the Detroit Publishing Company, became highly successful making stereographs for people to look at in their parlors. The content of these stereographs ranged from admirals to machine shops to zinc mines. They were meant to educate and entertain. The important thing to remember, though, is that all the stereographs were designed to give people what they wanted to see. Exactly what they wanted to see. So to a society that was plagued by racial injustice, exploitation of labor, homelessness, and the abuse of women and children but that did not want to see or believe in any of that, stereograph makers sold pictures like the one on the next page.

Cincinnati, Ohio: The Whiting View Company, c1900. (Published with a highly offensive caption.) Library of Congress.

This may not be the kind of photograph you want to show your students, but it does clearly illustrate bias that is dictated by the purpose of the image, even without its offensive caption. To expose that bias we have only to ask ourselves one question. Which is likelier—that this child of 6 or 7 is deliriously happy picking cotton in the hot sun all day or that someone paid him a few cents to pose with a smile? Or perhaps he was told by the person employing him and his family to smile and was afraid not to. He might even have been quite happy for the opportunity to stop working and pose. The bias of the photograph is in the implication that African American children loved picking cotton.

As a primary source, there is nothing wrong with this photograph, so long as you remember the bias. There is information to be found in it and questions to be asked. How old do you think this child is? What is the child doing? What is he wearing? What do you think work like this would be like? Why do you think photographs such as these were created? Doing a little research and grouping the photo with an excerpt from an oral history and a secondary source about African American life in the South or the process of picking cotton at this time would be very revealing.

You should also be aware that similar photographs, though usually more subtle than this, are still used today to depict life in slavery. In our decades of research into historical photographs of African Americans, we have discovered that there are almost no photographs of enslaved people at work in plantation fields. Virtually the only extant photographs of enslaved people were taken by the Union soldiers who were liberating them, and those were usually group portraits taken in front of the plantation house or some other plantation building. The only exceptions were occasional photographs of nannies and other house slaves taken with slave-owning families. In other words, if you see a photograph that purports to be an enslaved person at work in a field, you should have grave doubts that it actually is. The photograph of the boy in the cotton field above, as the caption says, was taken 35 years after the end of the Civil War.

A subtler, but equally common example of bias in the stereograph world, and in many other pictures, is the nostalgic and sentimental depiction of idyllic childhood. For many years childhood—at least for middle class white children—looked like the photo on the right.

This idyllic view of childhood was widespread for one particular era in American history, stretching from the late nineteenth century to the middle of the twentieth century. It was bolstered by the careful selection of images that were published in magazines and newspapers, in advertisements, and on greeting cards. These images were sometimes manipulated and sometimes not, but they shaped our vision of childhood by default because images of all kinds of children in all kinds of situations were simply missing. These photographs of idyllic childhood stood in a contrast to the photographs taken by social reformers who photographed childhood betrayed. Those photographs, however, were not so widely distributed and did little to change the stereotype.

The contemporary equivalent of the stereograph photos might very well be stock photos. They're everywhere, in our magazines, on television, on posters in our banks, even in our textbooks—and they show us a world that doesn't exist. Though some stock houses and photos are edgier, the vast majority show a sanitized version of the world. In that world, the models pretend to be doctors and mothers and grocery store clerks. They pretend to be constructing buildings and having parties and applying for jobs. They are prettier and better dressed than people in the real world simply because they are models and are frequently dressed by stylists. Their houses and offices are cleaner and their lawns are greener. And the prejudices of our society are built into the photos.

Photograph purchased from an antique store. Judging from the photograph type and internal evidence, it was taken in the 1920s. Austin/Thompson Collection.

Stock images have a bias that is very similar to that of the stereograph photos, with a little twist. They are not usually sold to individuals to look at in the parlor, and they do not even pretend to have an educational component. But they are used to sell other things—from toothpaste to money market accounts—and they are used because they are cheap to buy, easy for the viewer to digest and decode, and often because they represent a version of reality in places where reality itself might be considered disturbing or unattractive. Unfortunately, like the stereographs of a century ago, they also shape our sense of what the world is by what they show and what they don't show.

Bias is often revealed in what we don't see, as in the case of the pictures of childhood mentioned above. This issue is probably too complex for younger children, but for upper-level students it can be an interesting area to explore. When we began work on the book *The Face of Our Past: Images of Black Women from Colonial America to the Present,* we assumed that there were few available images of African American women in the archives. That's because we didn't see them in the history books. We didn't see them in mainstream history books, in African American history books, or in women's history books. They simply were not there. And this was not in the days of Jim Crow. It was in 1999. The civil rights and women's movements were decades old. If black women were not visible in the history books, it only made sense to us that it was because—for reasons of race, class, and gender discrimination—they had not been photographed.

However, when we began our research, we found photographs of black women everywhere. There were thousands, maybe tens of thousands of them in archives and museums around the country. So why weren't they in the books? Because the books were written by people who had a bias. The bias was probably unconscious in most cases, but it was there. The writers and editors just didn't think black women were important to the history they, the writers and editors, were writing.

Manipulation of the Source

Bias can manifest itself in the editing of a source as well as the creation of it. A potent example to bring up with older students is the diary of Anne Frank. Anne Frank wrote her diary but she wasn't alive to choose whether or what parts of the diary should be published. Her father edited her diary and didn't include many entries where Anne wrote about sex or wrote less than kind or flattering descriptions of the people in her life. For example, Otto Frank understandably did not include an entry where Anne wrote, "Father's fondness for talking about farting and going to the lavatory is disgusting." (A complete version of Anne Frank's diary was published in 1996 after her father's death.) This example, instructive and memorable as it is, may not be something you want to use with your students. For classroom purposes, you could give your students this example. Anne wrote about their helper Bep's getting engaged. She says that the family isn't happy about it because they don't think Bep loves her future husband. Otto Frank removed that entry because Bep was still alive and he didn't want to hurt her feelings.

Often, material will be edited for use in textbooks. Excerpts will be chosen for their level of readability, for example, and difficult sections edited out. A photograph can also be edited. Photographs are often cropped before they are published, sometimes to fit space requirements and sometimes to make a better composition. But it is also possible to crop something out of a photograph that someone does not want us to see. A famous example of this is Stalin's systematic removal of his political enemies from official photographs. Visual examples of this can be found by doing a simple Internet search. For example, a University of Minnesota web page shows the removal of Trotsky from some Soviet photographs.

Let's emphasize again that we are not saying that any of these sources are useless as sources of information. But the fact that both images and text can be manipulated points to the fact that it is dangerous to generalize from just one source. Remember, "if your mother tells you she loves you, . . . "

"The camera doesn't lie" has lost a lot of currency since the advent of Photoshop, but a photograph does not have to be significantly altered to show the bias of the photographer. A few harsh shadows can make a kind, compassionate person look like a villain. A few pretty props and a soft focus can make a selfish lout look like an angel. Most photographic bias, of course, is much subtler than that, but having a little bit of visual literacy can be very valuable in looking at a primary source photograph as well as cartoons, drawings, and other forms of art that we intuitively feel would be easier to "fudge."

For example, it is possible to change the effect of a photograph simply by lighting it differently.

Photographs of radio personality Mike Nowak. Photograph by Helen Tracy, 2013. Austin/Thompson Collection.

When asked to describe the character of the man on the left, viewers might use words like *kind* and *friendly*. The print on the right would be much more likely to elicit words like *tense, annoyed*, or even *sinister.*

The Crusaders

It is important that students understand that bias is not cheating. It can lead to cheating, of course. And it can lead to unconscious slanting. Or it can simply be the purpose and passion behind the creation of the image.

Many of the photographs that your students will be exposed to were taken by documentary photographers. Many of those photographers were crusaders against the ills of the nation. Their biases were against exploitation, against poverty, and against discrimination, and most of us are understandably sympathetic to their purposes. But their very passion for reform was a type of bias. Consider, for example, photographer Jacob Riis. Riis's bias was that street children were worthy of his (and our) attention and that they needed to be protected and saved. He took photographs that reflected this bias. Many people during that time period did not share Riis's bias. If they had, there would have been no need for him to take the photographs in the first place.

One thing to be aware of when looking at the images of Jacob Riis and Lewis Hine and other documentary photographers is selective publication. A good example is "the mill girl." Most students from at least fifth grade onward will be familiar with a Lewis Hine image of a mill girl or some other child worker from the early nineteenth century. Usually the image looks something like the one we show here.

A little spinner in the Mollahan Mills, Newberry, S.C., 1908.
Photograph by Lewis Hine. Library of Congress.

The image shows a small unhappy—or at least serious—girl, surrounded by large, potentially dangerous machines. It strongly supports the contention that child labor is bad and must be addressed. This image is certainly a "true" image. It hasn't been doctored or faked. It is an accurate and educational primary source.

Now compare that image with this one, also by Lewis Hine:

Noon hour, Brookside Cotton Mills, Knoxville TN, 1910. Photograph by Lewis Hine. Library of Congress.

This image shows a child running from the mill at lunchtime in 1910. It shows an aspect of life that was just as true for child workers as the drudgery and danger seen in the previous photograph—the joy of leaving work and palling around with friends. We have found in our presentations that it is an image that resonates with students today because they understand the joy it shows. However, the first kind of Hine image is the one that is used almost exclusively, not the second. The second image does not depict the dangers and negative elements of child labor, which Hine—and our textbooks—wish to depict. Again, this is not to say that Hine or the textbooks are wrong to use the sadder child labor images, just that bias is used in the selection.

The interesting thing in this case is that the photograph of the girl running makes it much easier for us to identify with her. She is not simply a pathetic victim. She is a person who smiles, who runs, and who is capable of enjoying herself. That makes her 10-hour shifts at the mill more, not less, painful to think about. In the classroom you could apply the strategies to each image and then have students compare and contrast them. Questions could include the following:

- How do you think each of these girls was feeling when she got her picture taken? Why did she feel that way?
- How do you feel looking at each of these photographs? Do you relate more to one than another?
- Does looking at both photographs change the way you think about children working in the mills?
- Why is the first photograph published more often than the second?*

A Case Study in Bias: The Farm Security Administration Collection

As we have seen, many primary sources contain some form of bias because they are created by human beings, and bias is a very human condition. Documentary photographers, such as Hine and Riis, have a clear bias as the very essence of their work. Sometimes an entire collection has a bias. Consider the Farm Security Administration (FSA) collection at the Library of Congress. This collection is the source of most of the photographs of the Great Depression you have seen, including what is often called "The Migrant Mother."

Florence Thompson, migrant worker, with three of her children, Nipomo, California, 1936. Photograph by Dorothea Lange for the FSA. Library of Congress.

*This kind of analysis meets standards about citing evidence, CCSS.ELA-Literacy.RI.4–8.1; explaining events and ideas in a historical text, CCSS.ELA-Literacy.RI.4–6.3; determining an author's purpose and bias, CCSS. ELA-Literacy.RI.4–8.6; drawing on information from multiple sources, CCSS.ELA-Literacy.RI.4–6.7; and comparing and contrasting two texts on the same topic, CCSS.ELA-Literacy.RI.3–8.9.

Or this iconic image of an oncoming dust storm.

Farmer and sons walking in the face of a dust storm. Cimarron County, Oklahoma, 1936.
Photograph by Arthur Rothstein for the FSA. Library of Congress.

The photographers of the FSA went out to find and record images showing poverty across the country. Their job was to touch the hearts and minds of the American people so that they would see the need for, and support, Roosevelt's New Deal programs. The FSA Historical Collection, headed by Roy Stryker, began in 1935 as a way to document the workings of the Resettlement Administration (RA) and its efforts to move the rural poor from submarginal to more productive land. Over time the mandate expanded to record small town America, industry, mining, and finally cities.

The very purpose of the FSA collection was to show hungry, unhappy people in need of government assistance and, on the other hand, the happy, healthy people who had received government assistance, like the girls pictured on the next page.

Children who live at Greendale, Wisconsin, 1939. Photograph by John Vachon for the FSA. Library of Congress.

These girls lived in a community in Greendale, Wisconsin, which was planned by the Suburban Division of the Resettlement Authority. In fact, for older students in grades 6 and up, telling the story of the FSA and then comparing and contrasting this image with the images above is an excellent way to look at and discuss visual bias. While telling the truth and portraying people's lives honestly, the FSA photographers were also fulfilling a very specific purpose and doing it with a clear bias.*

So we have bias based on the organizing mission of the FSA Historical Section, but we also have a bias based on another factor. You may have noticed that most famous images from the Depression are pictures of white people. And that's not because there were no poor or suffering people of color. It's not even because the photographers didn't take pictures of people of color. They did. It's because the images that were published were usually of white people.

Roy Stryker, the head of the Historical Division, once wrote to photographer Dorothea Lange, "Regarding the tenancy pictures, I would suggest you take both black and white, but place the emphasis on the white tenants since we know that

*This exercise would meet standards about explaining events and ideas, CCSS.ELA-Literacy.RI.6.3; determining an author's purpose and bias, CCSS.ELA-Literacy.RI.6–8.6; drawing on information from multiple sources and presented in different media, CCSS.ELA-Literacy.RI.6.7; and comparing and contrasting two texts on the same topic, CCSS.ELA-Literacy.RI.6–8.9.

these will receive much wider use." Unfortunately, the images of white people during the Depression still get much wider use. But the photographs of African Americans during the Depression are as powerful as any of the others.

Cairo, Illinois. May 1940. This young boy dances for arrivals at a hotel for 5 cents a dance.
John Vachon for the Farm Security Administration. Library of Congress.

In looking at an image of the FSA collection, then, we know that the photographer was hired to capture and record images that would make Roosevelt's New Deal programs look both necessary and effective. We know that the choice of which images were published was influenced by the racial biases of the time. These factors are important to remember when we encounter any image or piece of text. They answer the question, "Why was this source written/recorded/published?"

However, while the photographs from the FSA may have been intended as propaganda, they became something else. The photographers were among the best America has ever produced—Gordon Parks, Dorothea Lange, Walker Evans, Ben Shahn, Marion Post Wolcott, and others. As artists, they went beyond their purview and recorded life in America in its many forms. So we can also ask the question of an FSA photograph, "Does this fall within the bias of its mission?" Or does it transcend that mission to become a part of a great documentation of life in the United States?

Conclusion

In the contemporary world, bias is often talked about as though it were synonymous with prejudice or discrimination. In fact, it is a natural component of virtually all human communication. It is essential to be aware of bias and to take it into account when analyzing any primary source and to explore its effect on that source.

Things to Think About

1. Are you usually aware of bias in what you read or view?

2. Are you aware of biases other than political bias?

3. How much do you think images such as stock photos affect our view of the world and ourselves?

4. Would providing more variation in the images your students see and the voices they read affect the way they think?

Just for Fun

Give your students a question on which different people would have different opinions. For example, "Should workers in restaurants get paid more?" Then have volunteers choose roles, such as restaurant owner, waitperson, and customer. Have them express their opinion on the question without revealing the role they've chosen. Then ask the class to guess which role each person selected.

More Fun

To help students understand the effect of lighting, have them do the flashlight under the chin experiment. Have students assume sweet, gentle, or happy expressions. Then, while they keep the same expression, darken the room and have students light a flashlight under their chins. How sweet, gentle, or happy do they look now?

Chapter Six
Strategy 4: Examine Closely the Source Itself

Strategy 1: Decide what you're looking at.

Strategy 2: Determine the purpose and audience.

Strategy 3: Look for bias.

Strategy 4: Examine closely the source itself.

Strategy 5: Find more information.

Strategy 6: Consider your own role in the interaction.

Strategy 7: Compare a variety of sources.

In many ways, close examination is the most interesting, exciting step in the process of interpreting visual primary sources. Roughly analogous to close reading or identifying supporting details in text, close examination means really looking at all the details of the material carefully and creatively. It involves finding and interpreting clues to the reality being portrayed. If dealing with a primary source is detective work, this is examining the crime scene. It involves keeping in mind what you decided was the purpose of the material and its intended audience and interpreting details in light of that. During this process, you will also formulate questions that you hope to answer by going further and further into the source. It also involves forming questions for additional research, which is the next strategy.*

An excellent way to approach close examination of a photograph is to introduce an image to students without any identifying caption or source information. Work with students to determine what can be discovered just by looking at the image closely. How much students can identify on their own and how much you help them will depend on age and grade level, as will the level of sophistication of the details noted.

Snapshots can be a fun way to begin looking closely at an image because sometimes the only information we have about a snapshot is what can be gleaned from close examination. The image on the next page is just such an example.

---

*Discussions and activities in this chapter prepare students to meet standards about reading closely, CCSS. ELA-Literacy.CCRA.R.1; asking and answering questions and citing evidence, CCSS.ELA-Literacy.RI.K–8.1; determining an author's purpose and point of view, CCSS.ELA-Literacy.RI.K–8.6; and how that purpose shapes content, CCSS.ELA-Literacy.CCRA.R.6.

Photograph purchased on eBay. Austin/Thompson Collection.

First, we apply Strategy 1 and identify the photograph as a snapshot. Strategy 2 tells us that the audience for the snapshot is probably family and friends and the purpose is to record a moment in the lives of the children. In applying Strategy 3, we decide that the only bias in the photograph is the tendency on the part of the photographer to think these kids are cute and worth recording.

Next, we examine the clues (details) from the focus of the image.

The focus of the image is five children. We can look closely at them and note the details. The boy on the left appears to be wearing a costume of some kind, perhaps a version of the frontiersman's (or Native American's) buckskin. All the children have hats on. Two of the boys are wearing overalls. Two of the children are in wagons. One wagon has "Ford" written on it. The two children in wagons are wearing heavy coats. One is wearing a scarf. All the children seem to have shoes on. None of the clothing looks terribly worn, (except what might be a tear on the pants of the boy on the left) but the clothes do not look fancy or expensive.

Then we need to find clues from areas of the image that are not the focus. For this using a grid system might be helpful.

The upper left section shows a wooden building (clapboard house) and a sapling. It looks like there is another structure behind the clapboard house. The bottom left section shows grass and the edge of a path or sidewalk. The upper center section shows trees with no leaves. It also shows another building. There is a pointed roof above the little girl's head. Could it be a steeple? The lower center shows a sidewalk or path and shadows from the wheels of the wagons. The upper right side of the photo shows a few more buildings at a distance and trees with no leaves. The lower right shows more grass. No street is visible.

Now that we have really looked at the photograph and identified the clues we can begin to ask questions such as who, where, and when and see how many can be answered.

Who: At its most basic this image shows a group of children who lived at some point in the past. Older students could be directed to consider the children's class: The clothing, the fact that some of the children are wearing coats, and the apparent good condition of most of the clothing indicates that the children are not terribly poor.

Where: At its most basic we know from the clues that this is not a city. Due to the number and placement of the buildings, it doesn't *seem* like a farm. It could be a small town. (The sapling might be a clue that the clapboard house is a new building and that this photo was taken in a newly built suburban area, but that's tenuous and demands a level of knowledge most students won't have.)

When: Younger students should be able to place this image in the past. Considering the clues about the clothing and trees, they should be able to place this image as being taken in the fall, winter, or early spring. They should also be able to compare and contrast their own toys and clothes with the clothes and toys in the photograph. Older students might use the clue "Ford" written on the wagon to determine that this image was taken after the introduction of Ford cars. The shadows under the wagons indicate that it was a sunny day, and probably near the middle of the day. For older students, certain clues in the image could be researched in order to more specifically date the photo. They could find out when Fords became popular (1908) and when wagons such as the ones in the photo were made. (For more on research and images, see Chapter Seven.)*

Consider this photograph of a little girl in Rochester, New York:

A young girl with a fur bonnet, scarf, and muff looks in a toy shop window. Photograph by Albert Stone. Printed in Rochester Herald, December 13, 1919, Courtesy of Rochester Images, Monroe County Library System.

*This exercise meets standards about reading closely, CCSS.ELA-Literacy.CCRA.R.1; asking and answering questions and citing evidence, CCSS.ELA-Literacy.RI.K–8.1; and can be used to introduce students to comparing and contrasting skills, CCSS.ELA-Literacy.RI.K–6.9.

This image could be used as early as kindergarten and first grade. The caption tells us that this is a news photograph, printed in the Rochester Herald in 1919. Since it does not portray a newsworthy event, its purpose was to show the life of the community. You might say it has a bias in terms of showing an idyllic view of childhood.

Now, begin asking your students questions that elicit the most general information first: *What does this image show?* A little girl. *Is this picture from the present or from the past?* The past. *How can you tell?* Her clothes are different from the clothes people wear today. *What is the girl doing?* She's looking in a store window. Then move into looking more closely at the picture. You can now ask questions that point out or elicit details. *Can you describe what the girl in this picture is wearing?* Dress, boots, some kind of stockings that come down over her boots, a coat, a fur hat and collar. *How are her clothes like what you or your friends wear and how are they different?* Possible responses: I wear shoes, but mine look different. I usually wear pants, not dresses. If you can, zoom in on the picture.

What can you see in the store window? Toys, the girl's reflection. *Does the caption help you understand what type of store it is?* Yes. *Can you tell what any of the toys are?* Maybe a toy boat, but the rest I can't see. *Are the girl's clothes and the toys in the window like your clothes and toys? How are the same, and how are they different?**

---

*This exercise meets standards about reading closely, CCSS.ELA-Literacy.CCRA.R.1; asking and answering questions and citing evidence; CCSS.ELA-Literacy.RI.K–8.1; using features to locate information, CCSS.ELA-Literacy.RI.1–3.5; and can be used to introduce students to comparing and contrasting skills, CCSS.ELA-Literacy. RI.K–6.9.

Expect the Unexpected

It's very easy to see only what you're looking for. Even the most scholarly historians become so fond of their own ideas that they sometimes see only what supports those ideas. That's why Strategy 4 is so important. Your students need to train their minds and their eyes to see what's actually in a primary source, the unexpected something that is so revealing. One of our favorite examples of this is a photo of children standing in a shack during the Depression.

We can apply Strategies 1, 2, and 3 by reading the caption and quickly glancing at the image. It is from the FSA so it is a social documentary photograph, the purpose of which is to garner support for New Deal policies from its audience, the American public. In the last chapter, we dealt at length with the complex bias of the FSA photographs. As for the other questions, (who?) the photo shows unnamed, poor African American children; (when?) June, 1941; (where?) Caroline County, Virginia.

Ten people live in this shack. They must move to make way for the Army maneuver grounds. Caroline County, Virginia, June 1941. Photo by Jack Delano for the Farm Security Administration. Library of Congress.

It's a powerful image, and using the focus and grid system we can find many details that will add depth to our understanding of it. What makes this image one of our favorites, though, is in the lower right section. This photograph, unlike most photographs, can answer how. Look closely at this section of the photo.

There is a cable running along the ground into the shack! Now, go back and look at the angle and brightness of the light on the children's faces. Look at the sharpness of the shadows.

These two details show us that the photographer seems to have run a cable into the shack and set up a light. Otherwise the children inside the shack would probably not be visible. Certainly they would not be so brightly lit.

This wonderful detail can be used in many ways. Teachers of lower grades can use this photograph to explore the science of light and shadow. Upper grade teachers can use the close examination of this photograph to lead students to a deeper level of *why*. Students can be engaged in a discussion of how images communicate. Why did the photographer do this? How does having the children in the shack help us understand the size of the shack or the children's poverty? Was the photographer right to do this? Could the photographer have also "arranged" the tipped over washtub? Why would he do that? Does arranging the people and the lighting make a photograph less true?

Obviously this photograph could be used while teaching the history of the Great Depression. Close examination also showed us that it could be used to teach the science of light and shadow. But most importantly, the close examination of the photo demanded the use of key critical thinking skills.*

---

*This exercise meets standards about reading closely, CCSS.ELA-Literacy.CCRA.R.1; asking and answering questions and citing evidence, CCSS.ELA-Literacy.RI.K–8.1; determining an author's purpose, CCSS.ELA-Literacy.RI.K–8.6; and how that purpose shapes content, CCSS.ELA-Literacy.CCRA.R.6.

Close Examination of Text

Of course the same skills can be applied to textual as well as visual primary sources. To start students on a "case," find a text primary source with some good and interesting clues. For example, here is a piece of text.

> *Rose at five. The sun was shining brightly through my window, and I felt vexed with myself that he should have risen before me; I shall not let him have that advantage again very soon. How bright and beautiful are these May mornings! The air is so pure and balmy, the trees are in full blossom, and the little birds sing sweetly. I stand by the window listening to their music, but suddenly remember that I have an Arithmetic lesson which employes me until breakfast; then to school, recited my lessons and commenced my journal. After dinner practised a music lesson, did some sewing, and then took a pleasant walk by the water. I stood for some time admiring the waves as they rose and fell, sparkling in the sun, and could not help envying a party of boys who were enjoying themselves in a sailing boat. On my way home, I stopped at Mrs. Putman's and commenced reading "Hard Times," a new story by Dickens ... I anticipate to much pleasure in reading this story.—Saw some agreeable friends ... prepared tea, and spent the evening in writing.*

Read the piece of text with your students to get a sense of it. Then go through the text, gathering clues and applying the strategies.

Strategy 1: The clues tell us that this piece of text is probably a journal or diary entry. It could be a part of a letter, but there is no salutation and no inquiry into another person's well being. (i.e., "How are you and the family.") One clue that it's a journal is that the writer mentions writing in a journal. ("recited my lessons and commenced my journal.") Also, the style of chronologically recording the events and impressions of the day is a clue that this is a diary or journal.

Strategy 2: The audience is the writer of the journal. The purpose is to record the events and feelings of a day. There may be other purposes as well, including self-expression.

Strategy 3: Since a diary is not usually written for other people to read, there are only the writer's deeply felt and culturally ingrained biases, not any deliberate attempt to influence the reader.

Now, what other questions can be answered just from examining the text.

When: The clue "these May mornings" tells us the month. (Even without that specific information we could determine that it was written close to the summer solstice because the sun was up at 5 a.m.) The clue "'Hard Times,' a new story by Dickens" tells us the year. *Hard Times* was published in 1854, so this piece of text was written in May 1854.

Who: We know that this person is probably a young person because he or she is attending school. We know that this person is probably female because of the clue "did some sewing." In 1854, sewing was usually done by women and girls. We know that this person is probably part of the middle or upper class because she is attending school rather than working.

Where: There is not much information here about where the text was written. The text tells us that the writer was near the water and that there were trees and birds, which could describe a great many places.

So without any source information, the clues in the text tell us that this is a diary entry written by a middle or upper class girl in May, 1854, who lived near water. And in fact this is the Wednesday, May 24 entry from Charlotte Forten's diary, written while Charlotte was living in Salem, Massachusetts. It appears in an abridgment of the diary published by Capstone Press and entitled *Diary of Charlotte Forten: A Free Black Girl Before the Civil War.**

Of course, not all pieces of text will answer all these questions. Also, students will usually have source material that will provide the answers to at least some of those questions. But close examination of textual primary sources can be used to help students determine what is said explicitly and what can be inferred as well as to understand their own reactions and impressions from a piece of text.

Consider the following text:

U.S.S. Maine
Havana, Cuba

Dear Father,

I received your loving letter a few days ago and was pleased to hear from you. I would have written sooner but owing to us having to been ordered to sea so soon. I didn't have any chance. We are now in Havana Cuba. We arrived here yesterday after a five hour run around a place called Dry Tartogos a small Florida reef. We were out to sea when the orders came for us to proceed at once to Havana. We are the first American ship that has been here in six years. We are now cleared for action with every gun in the ship loaded and men stationed around the ship all night. We are also ready to land a battalion at any moment. By the looks of things now I think we will have some trouble before we leave. We steamed the whole length of Cuba and about every mile you can see puffs of smoke and the Spainards firing on the rebels. There are three German ships (?) loading. here was Old Moro Castle stands at the entrance of the harbor, there are thousands of Spanish inside you can see them all sitting on the walls at any time of the day. This

*This exercise meets standards about reading closely, CCSS.ELA-Literacy.CCRA.R.1; asking and answering questions and citing evidence, CCSS.ELA-Literacy.RI.4–8.1; and determining point of view, CCSS.ELA-Literacy. CCRA.R.6, CCSS.ELA-Literacy.RI.4–7.6.

is a landlocked harbor but I think we could get out of it all right although we are in a pretty dangerous position at the present time and we hardly know when we are safe. Well dear Father I will now have to close sending my best love and wishes to all and hoping that I may be alive to see you all again.

I remain you loving son. Charles

This is clearly a letter, a personal letter from a son to his father. With a small amount of additional research on the clue "USS *Maine*, Havana, Cuba," we can tell that this letter was written by Charles Hamilton sometime between January 25, 1898 when the *Maine* arrived in Havana and February 15th when the *Maine* sank. Details such as "a few days ago" and "yesterday" as well as frequent use of the present tense—"we are now cleared for action"—show us that the author is writing about very recent and current events. This is all very basic information.

This text, however, can be examined closely with students to discover a deeper level of who. Some of the errors, such as run-on sentences, sentence fragments, and errors of spelling show that the writer, Charles, was not highly educated. Yet despite these errors, he is able to communicate clearly and concisely. Therefore Charles is probably both smart and aware. Some details in the text show that he is observant, "about every mile you can see puffs of smoke" and "there are thousands of Spanish inside you can see them all sitting on the walls at any time of the day." Other clues in the text reveal him as thoughtful, "By the looks of things now I think we will have some trouble before we leave." Combining all the clues gives the reader an impression of Charles.*

Each reader will develop a slightly different impression of Charles as he or she examines the text, just as the reader might come to different conclusions upon close examination of an image. The point is not to find final, absolute truths, but to engage in close examinations and develop critical thinking skills that will lead to deeper understandings.

Conclusion

The motto of our website, OneHistory.org, is "The Truth Is in the Details." Closely examining a primary source is the way to find those details that lead you to the truth of history and a depth of understanding essential to comprehension.

---

*This exercise meets standards about reading closely, CCSS.ELA-Literacy.CCRA.R.1; asking and answering questions and citing evidence, CCSS.ELA-Literacy.RI.6–8.1; explaining events and ideas in a historical text, CCSS.ELA-Literacy.RI.K–6.3; determining the meaning of words and phrases in a text, CCSS.ELA-Literacy.RI.4–6.4.

Things to Think About

1. **What do you do now in your classroom that requires close attention to details?**

2. **How could students benefit from improving their skills of observations and analysis?**

3. **Do you think your students would find applying this strategy interesting and challenging? Would some of them find it frustrating?**

Just for Fun

Play this game. Put a dozen or more objects on a tray and cover it with a cloth. Remove the cloth for one minute and allow students to look at the objects. Then cover the objects again and see whether the class, working together, can name all the objects on the tray.

Chapter Seven
Strategy 5: Find More Information

Strategy 1: Decide what you're looking at.

Strategy 2: Determine the purpose and audience.

Strategy 3: Look for bias.

Strategy 4: Examine closely the source itself.

Strategy 5: Find more information.

Strategy 6: Consider your own role in the interaction.

Strategy 7: Compare a variety of sources.

The fifth strategy for examining a primary source is research, finding out more about the object you're looking at. Primary sources are excellent tools for research projects large and small. Several of the examples we've presented thus far have involved research, such as the image of Charles Nichols at the reform school. But even if your students are just looking at visual or textual primary sources in the textbook, research can be involved. Research also incorporates a number of critical thinking skills called out in the Common Core State Standards.*

There are sites and articles on how to help your students learn how to research, all with the same basic steps: plan/prepare, search, take notes, and present findings. We will not go into detail about how to teach researching. We will be discussing ways to apply research to text and images in order to find out more information and improve/apply critical thinking skills.

Much of what can drive additional research for a primary source can be connected to the "w" questions. If there are elements of who, what, where, when, and why that the surrounding text, caption, or attribution does not answer, there's an opportunity for research. Research can also be used to provide context. It's a way

---

*Discussions and activities in this chapter prepare students to meet standards about reading closely, CCSS. ELA-Literacy.CCRA.R.1; asking and answering questions, citing evidence, and drawing inferences, CCSS. ELA-Literacy.RI.K–8.1; describing the connection between two individuals, events, or ideas in a text as well as explaining events and ideas in a historical text, CCSS.ELA-Literacy.RI.K–6.3; determining the meaning of words and phrases in a text, CCSS.ELA-Literacy.RI.4–6.4; understanding the relationship between illustrations and the text in which they appear as well as drawing on information from multiple sources and presented in different media, CCSS.ELA-Literacy.RI.K–6.7; and comparing and contrasting key details from two texts, CCSS.ELA-Literacy.RI.4–6.9 and 8.9.

to extend students' knowledge and can involve closely reading or examining a primary source, solving mysteries, comparing sources for clues, and comparing and contrasting two sources in order to gather more information.

Search Tip

Google Image search results include photos from anywhere on the page where your search term appears, whether that image is connected to your search term or not. Always go to the page to determine how or if the image is connected to your search term.

If you search for the comedian Bud Abbott, for example, your image results could easily include a picture of Lou Costello. Or a search for Susan B. Anthony could yield a photograph of Elizabeth Cady Stanton.

Much of the research done by students today is via the Internet and Internet research is all about using good online databases and effective search terms. The website for your local public library probably has online dictionaries, encyclopedias, and other searchable databases your student can use. These should not be forgotten. SweetSearch, a search engine for students, has received generally positive press. For image research, your students will probably use Google Images, but it is extremely important to keep in mind—and to tell your students—that Google Images is only a place to *start*.

We will use Google Image searches in some of the examples in this chapter, but we are aware that, in order to avoid displaying potentially upsetting or inappropriate search results, many teachers use only educational sites. We would suggest that teachers of older students who are starting to prepare research projects spend some time explaining the dangers as well as the possibilities of Google Images because your students will probably be using the website at some point. Throughout this chapter we will be offering search term tips that can help you avoid the pitfalls and find information more easily.

Researching Visual Primary Sources

For the youngest students, simply connecting the text in a book to an image is a form of research. It is going from one place to another to find out information. Consider this image from the book published by Capstone, *A Baby Penguin Story:*

Out hatches a fluffy penguin chick. Cheep, chatter, peep! The tiny chick is hungry. Its mom spits up fish into its open mouth.

Show students just the image and engage them with a series of questions.

- What kind of animal is in this picture?
- What is happening in this picture?
- How do you know?

Reveal the text at the left and have (or help) students read it. Then ask them what they believe is happening in the picture. (The grown-up penguin is feeding fish to the baby penguin.) Young students can also participate in "true research." For example, students could participate in a class activity at the school library or use the Internet to find more pictures of baby penguins eating. An example such as this is probably safe for any level class. The first page of the Google Image results for the search term "baby penguin feeding" shows only appropriate images. Clicking on a few of the images can give students a larger view of the image without exposing them to any advertisements or content from the source web page. However, *always* check out search terms before using them with a class. For example, the search term "baby penguin feeding" resulted in benign, cute baby penguins eating from their parents' beaks. However, if you use the search term "penguin chicks eat," the results will include images of birds of prey eating baby penguins. This is not something your first grade class wants to see!*

---

*This exercise meets standards about reading closely, CCSS.ELA-Literacy.CCRA.R.1; asking and answering questions, CCSS.ELA-Literacy.RI.K–2.1; identifying the main topic or idea, CCSS.ELA-Literacy.RI.K–2.2; describing the connection between two individual, events, or ideas in a text CCSS.ELA-Literacy.RI.K–2.3; and understanding the relationship between illustrations and the text in which they appear, CCSS.ELA-Literacy.RI.K–2.7.

With older grades, the exploration and additional research about an image can be an adventure that really engages the class. Consider this image and caption:

A powder monkey standing on the deck of a ship.

As with all primary sources we start by looking at the image and reading the caption. When we apply Strategy 1, we run into problems. What kind of photograph are we looking at? It's a beautiful, clear image that doesn't look as though it is just a snapshot. It looks as though it was taken by a professional photographer. It's on the deck of a ship. The boy is wearing a kind of sailor's uniform, but is he actually a sailor, and why is someone taking his photograph? When we try to apply Strategies 2 and 3, these same questions prevent us from determining the audience, purpose, and bias of the photograph.

To truly know what this image is about requires research. We need to establish whether the caption is accurate and answer some other questions about this image. We can start out by looking for clues that will help us focus our search. A clue is something unusual or singular that will lead our thinking and our research in a particular direction.

We have an excellent clue in the caption: powder monkey. We need to find out what a powder monkey is. Any search engine leads to Wikipedia, which tells us that a powder monkey was a boy who took gunpowder from a ship's hold to the cannons on deck. Clearly, this is not a job that exists anymore. So, if this boy is actually a powder monkey, this is an old photograph.

SweetSearch provides a National Park Service site about powder monkeys, a free e-book novel about a powder monkey, *and* a link to this very photograph from the Library of Congress (LOC). Success! The LOC owns the photo, and it tells us that this picture was taken on the *USS New Hampshire* in Charleston Harbor between 1864–65. But can we find out more about the photograph or even about the boy pictured using that same clue?

A Google Images search using the term "powder monkey" reveals that this is the most common picture of a powder monkey on the Internet. Down the page we see a stereograph version of the image. It's very eye-catching. This is *clearly* an old version of the image. This version is from Wikimedia Commons and the attribution is the New York Public Library Digital Collections (NYPL). However, the NYPL says that this is a picture of a powder monkey on the *Pawnee*, not the *New Hampshire*. We have two reputable institutions with contradictory information. The LOC says the *New Hampshire*, the New York Public Library says the *Pawnee*. Who's right? This is an excellent opportunity for additional research.

Examining Captions, Credits, and Attributions

The NYPL version of the photo shows us the complete stereograph, not just the image, as the LOC does. The front of the stereograph contains the words "The War for the Union" and "Photographic History." On the back is text that names the site of the photograph as the USS *Pawnee* and has some wonderful text about what powder monkeys do and that the image "is specially interesting to boys." So far this seems like the definitive source.

However that phrase "Photographic History" is a new clue. It's also a red flag. "History" usually refers to something that was created in the past. Why is this version of the photo called history? Using clues from the stereograph itself we can find out. The back of the stereo tells us that the publisher of the image is Huntington and Taylor. The search term "Taylor and Huntington stereograph" leads us back to the LOC, which informs us that John C. Taylor published a series of Matthew Brady photographs in the 1880s and 1890s. So while the image might be a primary source, the stereograph's caption is not. The caption might be accurate, but it was written up to 30 years after the event and not by someone who was present at the event.

Using Other Photographs as Research Tools

Other images can be excellent resources for additional research while also using comparing and contrasting skills noted in the Common Core State Standards. To solve our mystery, we need to compare other images of the *Pawnee* and *New Hampshire* to our photo of the powder monkey.

Search Tip

If you find an image in a digital archive, looking at other images marked as "near" it or connected to it will provide you with more context and sometimes even provide vital information. Check to see if there are ways to link to the lot, group, or series the image is from. In the case of the Library of Congress, you can also "browse neighboring items by call number."

Most digital archives have search functions that allow you to search the entire archive. For example, a search for the word "Pawnee" in the NYPL Digital Gallery reveals three stereographs of the ship. One is of the boy, another is of the quarterdeck of the ship, and the third of an admiral and his staff. The photograph of the quarterdeck of the Pawnee shows a cannon that is very similar to the one the powder monkey is standing in front of, but is not the same. This is not enough for us to make a determination. A search for *"New Hampshire"* turns up too many results and "USS *New Hampshire*" produces no results. Time to move on.

If you're at the image of the powder monkey on the LOC website, you have another option. The LOC allows us to look at all the images from a particular lot or group by clicking the link in "Item is from this group." Clicking that link below the thumbnail of the powder monkey takes us to a series of photographs, "Civil War naval vessels and naval personnel." This provides confirmation that the photograph was taken by famous Civil War photographer Mathew Brady or one of his staff. Their job was to document the war for the Union. We have completed Strategies 1, 2, and 3.

On the second page of images, two photographs are captioned as being of the USS *New Hampshire*. Looking closely and comparing these two images with "our" powder monkey, it is clear that they were taken at the same spot on the ship. The big cannon is the same, but more importantly the cutlasses hanging behind the figures are the same. Are there other clues in these images that could help us?

Close examination of the two new images provides a solution to our mystery. In the image on the right there is writing below the cutlasses.

Zooming in on that writing, as well as applying some "Brightness and Contrast" magic in a graphics program, reveals the words "Arms Chest" and "New Hampshire"!

Mystery solved! Through research, comparing and contrasting, and close examination, we have discovered that the caption for the photo, while limited, is accurate. We also now know that the photo shows the *USS New Hampshire* (what) and was taken in Charleston Harbor (where) in 1864 or 1865 (when). We have learned that powder monkeys were boys, usually between 12 and 14, who carried gunpowder from the magazines in a ship's hold to the cannons on deck (who). We know this is a Mathew Brady photograph. This tells us that the photograph was taken to document the war and was then used for sale later (why).*

*This analysis meets standards about reading closely, CCSS.ELA-Literacy.CCRA.R.1; asking and answering questions and citing evidence, CCSS.ELA-Literacy.RI.5–8.1; and comparing and contrasting key details from two texts, CCSS.ELA-Literacy.RI.4–6 and 8.9.

Extend the Research

But there is even more to learn. In the Google Images search results for "powder monkey," the second time the full stereograph appears is on a site called Civil War Talk. This is not an academic site, but the author's review of the image of the powder monkey reveals this fascinating tidbit of information: This boy is the "mascot" of the National Civil War Naval Museum in Columbus, Georgia, and his name was Aspinwall Fuller. Going to the museum's site gives us no new information, but doing a Google image search for Aspinwall Fuller leads us to the National Portal to Historic Collections. There, a picture of the powder monkey notes his name as Aspinwall Fuller. So a reputable site has confirmed the name. A commercial site that shows up in the same search notes that Aspinwall enlisted in 1864 in Baltimore and that he was the president of the Marine Engineer's Beneficial Association before he died in 1888. However the site has no footnotes or way to confirm its assertions.

Can we find out anything more about Aspinwall and what happened to him? Research about the USS *New Hampshire* tells us that the ship was launched on April 23, 1864. For two years it served as a hospital and supply ship near Charleston, SC. Further searches do not mention any battles or skirmishes, so it appears that Aspinwall Fuller did not participate in any battles during his career as a powder monkey.

There are a number of genealogy sites where we can look up Aspinwall. (It's important to choose a site that includes a view of the actual census page.) A quick search leads us to an Aspinwall Fuller in the 1880 census. (If his name had been John Smith or Thomas Brown, we would have been out of luck.) This Aspinwall is 29, making him about 13 at the time the picture was taken. There is no other Aspinwall Fuller mentioned in the censuses for 1860–1880, so this entry is probably our powder monkey. The census tells us that in 1880 Aspinwall was living with his mother at 24 Carmine Street in New York City and working as an engineer. This matches the information noted above that he was president of the Marine Engineer's Beneficial Association.

Now when we look at the photograph, we see Aspinwall Fuller, a 12 or 13-year-old boy, standing on the deck of the USS *New Hampshire* in Charleston Harbor, sometime between 1864 and 1865. He is a powder monkey, doing the very dangerous job of carrying gunpowder from the magazine where the powder is stored to the cannons on deck. He has a mother who is living. In 15 years he'll be single, live with his mother in New York City, and have become an engineer.

From this one photograph and one clue we have gone on an adventure that solved a mystery, taught us about powder monkeys, and introduced us to one historical boy who lived the experience.

Textual Primary Sources

All (or much) of the research process we explored with an image can be applied to text as well. Although textual primary sources often have more specific attributions, research can be used to fill in gaps, provide context, and extend knowledge. Research on a text can include looking up unknown words, consulting a map to find out where an event took place, looking up the author of a source, or finding out more about the subject being discussed in the text.

For upper grades, a teacher might consider this text excerpt:

> *I knew that the men were watching me. I could feel their eyes on my back. I must go on. One step, two steps. The grass was soft and thick under my feet. Three steps. "I am a Crow. I have the heart of a grizzly bear," I said to myself. Three more steps and then he charged!*
>
> *A cheer went up out of a cloud of dust. I had struck the bull on the root of his tail!*
>
> *—Chief Plenty-Coups*

Strategy 1: This reads like a story told to someone else, not a diary entry. It is some kind of narrative, perhaps a memoir or oral history.

Strategy 2: As a memoir or oral history, its purpose would be to record one person's experience of the past. Beyond that, we would need more information about the origins of the text.

Strategy 3: Again, to determine any bias, we need more information.

Strategy 4: When we examine the material, these questions arise:

- Who is Chief Plenty-Coups?
- What is this material describing?
- Who are the Crow?
- What is a "coup(s)"?
- When did this event take place?
- Where did this happen?
- Why did Chief Plenty-Coups strike a bull on the tail?
- Why and in what context did Chief Plenty-Coups write about this event?

The clues for our research are embedded in the questions: "Crow," "Chief Plenty-Coups," "coups." Even assuming we have absolutely *no* prior knowledge about Native American and Plains Indian life we can use research to answer all the questions listed above.

The search term "History of the Crow Nation" leads to numerous reputable sources on the history of the Crow people as well as information about the Crow today, essential for dispelling the "vanishing Indian" myth—the belief that Native Americans were and are disappearing. A quick search on the term *coup* provides a Merriam-Webster dictionary definition.

The questions about Plenty-Coups lead down fascinating paths. The first page of results from a basic search of "Chief Plenty-Coups" leads to sites that tell us Plenty-Coups was a chief of the Crow nation in Montana, he lived from about 1848 until 1932, he was the last traditional tribal chief of the Crow, and his log cabin, sacred spring, and farmstead are now part of the Chief Plenty-Coups State Park.

Already we can answer a number of questions: *Who are the Crow?* A Native American nation who lived on the Great Plains. *What is coups(s)?* A surprising and impressive victory or achievement. *Who is Chief Plenty-Coups?* An important chief of the Crow Nation. *Where did this event take place?* Probably somewhere in Montana, where Plenty-Coups lived. The search results also introduce us to the term *counting coups*, which we can follow up with a new search.

A quick search reveals that *counting coups* is getting close enough to an enemy during battle to touch or hit him with a hand weapon or "quirt" (coup stick). Two search results also either use or discuss ledger paintings, which can provide a fabulous visual and historical adventure for students.

We still don't know the context for this quote, though. Are we even certain that Chief Plenty-Coups said these words? What more can we discover? The second page of our original search on "Chief Plenty-Coups" leads us to a free, full-text, online version of Plenty-Coups' "autobiography" and more answers. By using an exact phrase from our quote, we can quickly locate it in the broader text. This gives us confirmation of origin as well as context and a fuller, more detailed description. Our quote describes a moment when a 9-year-old Chief Plenty-Coups is participating in a rite of bravery. Plenty-Coups along with other boys his age were challenged by the elders of their tribe to touch a wounded and angry buffalo on the root of its tail. Any that could achieve the feat would be ready to count coups. (Be aware that in this case the description of the buffalo's wounds and torment is quite vivid and might be upsetting to some students.)

Now we know when the event took place (about 1857), what it is describing (a bravery challenge), why Plenty-Coups struck a bull on the tail (to show he was brave and ready to count coup), why Plenty-Coups wrote about this event (to describe the life of the Crow before the European settlement of his land), and in what context Plenty-Coups wrote about the event (the story was not written directly by Plenty-Coups but rather is Plenty-Coups' response to questions asked by Frank Linderman).

In this case, the additional material we have discovered provides myriad opportunities for building knowledge on subjects such, as bravery rituals and the importance of the buffalo in the life of the Plains Indians. Students also now have access to an entire book about Chief Plenty-Coups. Reading the entire book or portions of it could generate discussions about comparing and contrasting texts, authors' (both Plenty-Coups' and Linderman's) points of view, and authors' and reader's bias (see Chapters Five and Eight for more on this).*

---

*This exercise meets standards about reading closely, CCSS.ELA-Literacy.CCRA.R.1; asking and answering questions and citing evidence, CCSS.ELA-Literacy.RI.4—8.1; explaining events and ideas in a historical text, CCSS.ELA-Literacy.RI.4—6.3; determining the meaning of words and phrases in a text, CCSS.ELA-Literacy. RI.4—6.4; and drawing on information from multiple sources and presented in different media, CCSS.ELA-Literacy.RI.4—6.7.

Revisiting the Source

Once you have researched your primary source, it's time to return to it and see what new information you can see or understand. This second, more informed look may reveal details you and your students didn't even notice the first time. And it will certainly lead you to different conclusions about some of the things you did see the first time.

We often take a second or third look at an image or a text. This is automatic and we are not particularly aware we're doing it or that our impressions have changed. Who hasn't read a quote, come to a conclusion about it, then read the attribution and revised that conclusion, all in the space of moments. Or been familiar with an image, known its basic subject matter, and then found out more contextual information that made us see the image differently. Breaking this process down and making it explicit for students, however, can allow them to approach their analysis systematically and with care.

Every primary source can benefit from a second more informed look. We have utilized second and third looks already in this book, our earlier example of Charles Nichols in the reform school serving as a prime example. And like the photo of Charles Nichols, some primary sources are more effective examples than others of how information can drastically affect what we see in an image or what we understand about a piece of text.

Returning for a second look is exceptionally effective with students in younger grades. For example, remember the picture of the penguin adult and chick? You showed your students the photograph and asked them what they saw. Students might have responded that the momma penguin and baby penguin are kissing or talking.

Then you showed them the text and helped them read it, and you looked at other images of penguins feeding chicks. Now you can return to the photograph and look at it again. Can students "see" that the adult penguin is feeding the chick? What do they think will happen next? Will the chick stick its head in the adult's mouth like some of the other pictures they saw? What is hanging below the chick's mouth? Is that some food?*

---

*This analysis meets the standards for describing the relationship between illustrations and the text and how illustrations and text work together to convey information CCSS.ELA-Literacy.RI.K–3.7.

In the upper grades, you might start with some startling and dramatic examples of the strategy of researching and then revisiting the primary source. This will make it easier to understand when applied to subtler instances. Your students can also get a sense of the range of possibilities that this level of interpretation allows.

One dramatic example might be this photograph:

Chiricahua students at the Carlisle School, ca. 1886. Denver Public Library.

Starting with this image, students can examine the source, apply the first four strategies, make notes about their initial conclusions, and try to answer as many of the "w" questions as possible. A close examination of the expressions might inspire students to think that the students are serious, unhappy, angry, proud, stiff, or any number of other adjectives. Research about the image using information from the caption reveals that these students were Native Americans who had been sent to a school from Fort Marion, Florida, where they had been held in the prison there. The Carlisle School was created to assimilate Native Americans into European American culture. Students' searches will lead them to the photograph's companion:

Chiricahua Apaches as they arrived at Carlisle from Fort Marion, Florida, ca. 1886. Denver Public Library.

Students can then return to the first image with these questions in mind.

- Has anything changed about the image?
- Do you notice anything new in the image?
- Do the subjects expressions or stances seem to communicate anything different? Why or why not?

Students can now look back at the first image with informed eyes. New interpretations of the first image might include that the subjects of the photograph look uncomfortable (they are unused to the tight uniforms of the school), and more students might identify the subjects as looking sad or angry.

With this particular example, students can also compare and contrast the two images, which will inform how they see the students in the first picture. They can do additional research to discover why such before and after images were taken, who their intended audience was, and how that intended audience might have viewed the pair of images. Finally, students can think about how people today might view the pair of images and compare and contrast the reactions across time. This re-examination would then ask students to examine their own point of view, which will be addressed in more detail in the next chapter.*

---

*This exercise meets standards about reading closely, CCSS.ELA-Literacy.CCRA.R.1; citing evidence and drawing inferences, CCSS.ELA-Literacy.RI.4–8.1; explaining events and ideas in a historical text, CCSS.ELA-Literacy. RI.4–6.3; determining an author's purpose and bias, CCSS.ELA-Literacy.RI.4–8.6; integrating visual information with other information in print and digital texts, CSS.ELA-Literacy.RH.6–8.7; evaluating arguments and claims made in a text, CCSS.ELA-Literacy.CCRA.R.8; and comparing and contrasting key details from two texts and analyzing relationships between primary and secondary sources, CCSS.ELA-Literacy.RI.6–8.9.

Another way to explore how research and new knowledge influence how we interpret what we see and read might be to show your students a photograph with very little internal information, particularly one that might induce students to make snap judgments or to oversimplify. This should be an image that with even basic Internet research will yield interesting results. The image should be connected to an important historic event. The information from the research will then dramatically inform the way the photo can be examined and at the same time will introduce the student to a new element of human history.

Edward Hoyt, Orphan Train Rider, ca. 1912.

Consider the photograph to the left. Ask students to do a close examination of the photo. Have them make notes with their conclusions about the photograph and the boy pictured. (Possible conclusions might be that this is a studio photograph. It shows a rich boy who is healthy, content, and well cared for.)

Then have students conduct a straightforward Internet search using the name of the boy, Edward Hoyt, and the term "orphan train." These searches will lead students to sites that explain that the orphan train was a program from 1854 through 1929 that took more than 200,000 children from orphanages or the streets of New York and placed them with families in the rural Midwest. They will learn that some orphan train riders were treated as slave labor or were abused, while others became members of their foster families and still others were formally adopted. They will also find a website that details Edward Hoyt's story in particular. (For more information about the orphan trains, you could look at Capstone's *Orphan Trains: An Interactive History Adventure*.)

Edward's story is an orphan train tale with a happy ending; however, he had a hard beginning. He was born and lived his early life in Brooklyn, New York. His mother died of tuberculosis when he was

3 years old. His grandmother died in a fire that destroyed their apartment when he was 4, and when he was 5 his father left him at a boarding house along with his 7-year-old brother and 4-year-old sister. Then his father disappeared. The boarding house owner placed Edward and his siblings in an industrial school, where they would be trained in a trade. Just over two years later the brothers were sent on an orphan train to Valley Falls, Kansas.

After reading about the orphan trains and Edward's experience as a boy, have students revisit the photograph.

- Has anything changed about the image?
- Do you notice anything new in the image?
- Does the subject's expression or stance seem to communicate anything different? Why or why not?

At this point, students might feel differently about the boy in the picture. Some may find him easier to identify with. Some students who thought he looked a little smug before may now think he just looks lucky.*

With a carefully chosen piece of text, you and your students can have much the same experience as we have described with photographs. Consider this excerpt:

> *Slept in a paper box. Bummed swell breakfast three eggs and four pieces of meat. Hit [up] guy in big car in front of garage. Cop told me to scram. Rode freight to Roessville. Small burg, but got dinner. Walked Bronson. N. G. Couple a houses. Rode to Sidell. N. G. Hit homes for meals and turned down. Had to buy supper 20 cents. Raining.*

A close reading of the text yields some clues. Cars were in use. There is a reference to "riding a freight," something that we connect with the Great Depression. If we add an attribution, this information is confirmed but our perception of the text may change. This text comes from *Boy and Girl Tramps of America* (1934). If we thought it was a man before, we now know it is a boy. This is not an adult, not the stereotypical "hobo" character, with whom we're familiar. This is a kid—a kid who sleeps in paper boxes and is getting rousted by the cops. If the text seemed sad before, it seems doubly so now.

What happens to this piece of text if we add some research? If we research the title of the source, we hit pay dirt. A portion of this text is available online via the University of Virginia. The quote from our boy is not there, but the story of how and why our quote was recorded adds information and context. Thomas Minehan, the author, was a graduate student studying sociology who decided to ride the rails and travel with the homeless during the Depression, and then to focus on the children and youth traveling the country. Many of the quotes on this site are chilling and heartbreaking. They talk of abuse and neglect at home, but also of parents in poor

---

*This exercise meets standards about reading closely, CCSS.ELA-Literacy.CCRA.R.1; citing evidence and drawing inferences, CCSS.ELA-Literacy.RI.4–8.1; explaining events and ideas in a historical text, CCSS.ELA-Literacy. RI.4–8.3; determining an author's purpose and bias, CCSS.ELA-Literacy.RI.4–8.6; integrating visual information with other information in print and digital texts, CSS.ELA-Literacy.RH.4–8.7; and comparing and contrasting key details from two texts and analyzing relationships between primary and secondary sources, CCSS.ELA-Literacy. RI.4–8.9.

health and without work. After reading these quotes, our quote might seem even more poignant. The fact that he is young certainly seems less unique, less startling.

Some further searches yield nothing. The term "children hopping freights" largely provides results about modern young people who ride freight trains. Searching using the term "children tramps Depression" finally leads to the wonderful website, Riding the Rails, created by Errol Lincoln Uys, which is about his book of the same name. On Uys' site we can read more about the lives of children who hopped freight trains, and we learn that there were a quarter of a million of them!

Finally, we search trying to find more about the quote itself. Using a term from the quote, "bummed a swell breakfast," we find a chapter of a book posted on a history teacher's website. This is a good example of why it is important to run searches yourself before you assign them to students. There are graphic details in the chapter that could be disturbing to your students. It reveals that our quote is from a boy named Blink, so named because he lost an eye when a live cinder blew into his face while he was riding in an open car. Blink's suffers an open wound from the accident. He is riding the rails because he ran away from an abusive father. The quote is from a diary that Blink showed Minehan.

> **Cogent Quotation**
> The outcome of any serious research can only be to make two questions grow where only one grew before.
> —Thorstein Veblen

Now we can return to the quote. Our research has made the text more immediate, more real somehow. The lone boy speaker is now surrounded by hundreds of thousands of others. But he is also now a unique individual. He has a name, Blink. He's hurt. He puts in the effort to keep a diary, even while hopping freights. And one day he had a really good breakfast. Man, that breakfast sounds like a feast*

Conclusion

From an interesting image with a basic caption or a few isolated, interesting words with a simple attribution we have been able to identify clues, pursue leads, answer questions, solve mysteries, and discover exciting and interesting new material. You can use these examples with your students or find examples of your own (or use some of the examples we provide in Chapter Ten). Presenting your students with primary sources to investigate and research will engage and challenge them. They will have to think critically, examine closely, and analyze carefully. And perhaps they will experience how new knowledge can change perceptions.

---

*This exercise meets standards about reading closely, CCSS.ELA-Literacy.CCRA.R.1; citing evidence and drawing inferences, CCSS.ELA-Literacy.RI.6–8.1; and determining an author's purpose and bias, CCSS.ELA-Literacy.RI.6–8.6.

Things to Think About

1. What kinds of research do the students in your class already do?

2. How can you help your students view research more as a treasure hunt and less as a chore?

Chapter Eight

Strategy 6: Consider Your Own Role in the Interaction

Strategy 1: Decide what you're looking at.

Strategy 2: Determine the purpose and audience.

Strategy 3: Look for bias.

Strategy 4: Examine closely the source itself.

Strategy 5: Find more information.

Strategy 6: Consider your own role in the interaction.

Strategy 7: Compare a variety of sources.

Close examination of any image or text requires that the viewer bring to bear a lot of prior knowledge and personal experience. When we look at or read a primary source, we're really having a conversation with it. We bring our own experience to the item, and it gives us back various kinds of information. When you look at the scenery in a picture, you notice whether it's inside or outside, hot or cold, city or country. Then, everything you know about a hot, city room or a cool, country road helps you to understand what the photograph is trying to say to you.* According to *Implementing the Common Core State Standards: A Primer on "Close Reading of Text,"* "Understand that while engaged in Close Reading lessons, students naturally use prior knowledge to deepen their comprehension of the text. Teachers should activate prior knowledge and build background knowledge when appropriate, while ensuring that students' examination of text is the central means of conveying information."

And, of course, we do this without even thinking about it. Visually, we interpret body language and facial expressions. In comparing an image with our own world, we "recognize" both what we have seen before and what we have never seen. A lot of this happens in a split second. We might not even be aware that it's happening, but it is. And even a momentary first impression can be a big part of the conversation that we're having with the source. Consider this photograph:

*Discussions and activities in this chapter prepare students to meet standards about reading closely, CCSS. ELA-Literacy.CCRA.R.1; asking and answering questions, citing evidence, and drawing inferences, CCSS. ELA-Literacy.RI.K–8.1; explaining the main topic or idea, CCSS.ELA-Literacy.RI.K–8.2; determining an author's purpose and bias, CCSS.ELA-Literacy.RI.K–8.6; evaluating the claims made in a text, CCSS.ELA-Literacy.RI. K–8.8; distinguishing fact from opinion, CCSS.ELA-Literacy.RH.6–8.8; and integrating information from more than one text, CCSS.ELA-Literacy.RI.4–5.9.

Two school girls: Lulu Todi, Sara Adams, profile Northwest California; Hupa Reservation, Humboldt County, 1907. Phoebe Apperson Hearst Museum of Anthropology.

Most of us, when we look at this image, see two girls who are unhappy about what is happening at the time the photograph is being taken. We interpret the expressions on their faces and the touch of one girl's hand on the other girl's back, which seems to be a comforting gesture. We don't know why the girls are unhappy. That's information we can't get from the image itself, but our prior knowledge and personal experience fill in a great deal. (In our research, we found that the girls in the photograph were being studied by a team of physical anthropologists at their reservation when the photograph was taken.)

Observation and interpretation based on prior knowledge is natural and instinctive, and it is also a skill that can be developed. As a teacher, it's your job to help your students apply their prior knowledge in ways they may not think to do on their own. Most of the questions we have suggested that you ask your students are ways to do that.

At the same time, you need to help students understand that when they look at or read a primary source, they are also "shaping" it. They are looking through a lens created by the cultural values, standards, and experiences of their twenty-first century world. The image on the next page can be used to bring this home to even the youngest students.

Boy in Baltimore, Maryland, January 1, 1898.

Contemporary students looking at this image are likely to interpret the boy's clothing as a sign that he is not masculine. If asked questions like, "What kind of activity do you think this boy likes?" they might very well leave out sports like baseball or football. Even after they've been told that in earlier times it was not unusual for boys to wear these clothes when they dressed up, they may very well continue to view the boy with this cultural bias and therefore misinterpret the image. The fact is that there is no information at all in the photograph about whether the boy liked sports.*

Other cultural biases include forms of racial, gender, and ethnic prejudices and preconceptions. We all have these biases and need to be aware of them. Otherwise, we will not be able to accurately interpret and gain information from primary sources.

People also have personal biases that are not necessarily shared by others in the culture. You can explain to students that a person in a picture might remind you of yourself or someone you know. If you see a person in a photograph who reminds

---

*This exercise meets standards about reading closely, CCSS.ELA-Literacy.CCRA.R.1; asking and answering questions, citing evidence, and drawing inferences, CCSS.ELA-Literacy.RI.K–8.1; explaining the main topic or idea, CCSS.ELA-Literacy.RI.K–8.2; and determining an author's purpose and bias, CCSS.ELA-Literacy.RI.K–8.6.

you of your favorite aunt, you bring memories of that person to what you see. You almost automatically think that the person in the photograph is probably kind and funny, like your aunt. If the person in the photograph reminds you of someone who was mean to you, you bring that, too.

Taking one's own personal and cultural biases into account is crucial in the close reading of all primary source material, as well as in completely experiencing and understanding literature, art, and the world. It is probably easier to explain that to students using an image as an example, although we bring our biases to textual sources too. Look, for example at this excerpt from an oral history taken in 1979, as part of the Southern Oral History Program Collection. The speaker is Alice P. Evitt.

> [B]efore I was married when I lived in Concord, a lot of the girls—I played organ a heap—and they'd come in at night—the mill hill; no strangers, people we knowed—and I'd play the organ and the fella lived right there, he'd pick the guitar and they'd dance. But no outsiders didn't come in. They enjoyed it. I never did dance, never did learn 'cause I'd always play the organ and I couldn't get a chance [laughter]. We'd enjoy that. A lot of times on Sunday, I'd play the organ. A crowd of us'd get together and we'd sing.

This is a good account of recreation among a group of mill workers. But one of the first things many people will notice about it is the grammar and diction. Like the lace collar on the boy in the photograph on the previous page, this way of speaking can trigger a prejudice, a cultural bias. That bias might make a reader decide that the person talking here is less than intelligent. But there is actually no evidence of that, only that she was not well educated—probably because she left school to work—and that she spoke as people in her region of the country spoke.

So what's the antidote for cultural and personal bias? As you might expect, it's knowledge. And that's where your role as teacher becomes so important.

A Matter of Opinion

To prepare students to deal with their own biases, you'll need to talk about fact and opinion. In investigating a primary source, certain things will be clear and factual. "There is a tree on the left side" is a factual statement. "That girl is happy" is an opinion. Students need to make that distinction. Beyond that, they need to understand that opinions about photographs and other primary sources can be quite useful, but only if they are *informed* opinions.*

So, what is an informed opinion? It's an opinion that is supported by evidence. That evidence can be from the image itself. "The girl looks happy because she has a big smile and she's kind of dancing around." Or the evidence can be historical information from the caption, another primary source, or a reliable secondary source. The same sources can indicate that an opinion is probably wrong or unfounded, as in the case of the boy with the frilly collar.

---

*This discussion prepares students to distinguish fact from opinion, as required in CCSS.ELA-Literacy.RH.6–8.8.

The crucial question for students to ask themselves—and for you to ask them—is "Why do you think that?" The answer may be surprisingly revealing. If a student says that the boy in the frilly clothes probably wouldn't do "boy things" like playing baseball, you ask, "Why do you think that?" The answer will almost certainly have something to do with the boy's clothes. That's your chance to deliver some knowledge that could change the opinion. You can explain that clothing for boys was different in the nineteenth century, that boys wore dresses until they were 4 or 5 years old. After that age, their dress clothes, at least, were designed to be fashionable and, to some degree, to show the wealth of their parents. Most important, children had almost no say in what they wore. Their parents chose their clothing, and the children wore them. (We're going to talk in the next chapter about doing additional research on a primary source, which may be necessary in order to confirm or challenge an opinion about an image or a piece of text.)

Better yet, you could read the caption to your students: "Baltimore, January 1, 1898. Three year old George Herman Ruth poses for a portrait in Baltimore in 1898 long before he was known as 'The Babe.'" Then tell your students that the boy in the photograph grew up to be one of the greatest baseball players of all time.*

Recognizing this kind of bias is important for more than just being able to interpret the sources. It helps students recognize that people have not always had the same expectations of boys and girls, men and women, that we do now. Attitudes and values have changed and can change again, about this and other issues in our society. It helps students to develop a genuine sense of history and, perhaps, of possibilities for the future.

As a teacher, you are outside the conversation your student is having with the primary source. Your job is to be a facilitator, but you need to take care that you don't inhibit the interaction. Your questions and suggestions can lead students to a greater understanding, but that should not be *your* understanding.

Conclusion

The conversation between students and a primary source involves activating prior knowledge and bringing life experiences to their analysis and interpretation. It is an opportunity for students to learn more about history and about themselves.

*This exercise meets standards about reading closely, CCSS.ELA-Literacy.CCRA.R.1; asking and answering questions, citing evidence, and drawing inferences, CCSS.ELA-Literacy.RI.K—8.1; describing the connection between two individuals, events, or ideas in a text, CCSS.ELA-Literacy.RI.K—2.3; evaluating the claims made in a text, CCSS.ELA-Literacy.RI.K—8.8; and distinguishing fact from opinion, CCSS.ELA-Literacy.RH.6—8.8.

Things to Think About

1. Do you think your students are aware of personal bias at all?

2. How can you activate prior knowledge while keeping an awareness of possible bias?

Just for Fun

Do a search on the Internet for optical illusions and show them to your students as a way of demonstrating that we can't always trust what we think we see.

Chapter Nine
Strategy 7: Compare a Variety of Sources

Strategy 1: Decide what you're looking at.

Strategy 2: Determine the purpose and audience.

Strategy 3: Look for bias.

Strategy 4: Examine closely the source itself.

Strategy 5: Find more information.

Strategy 6: Consider your own role in the interaction.

Strategy 7: Compare a variety of sources.

No detective tries to solve a case with just one clue and no historian tries to create an account of a historical situation or event with just one source. The more independent sources you can look at, the closer you can get to what really happened*

In the classroom, looking at a variety of primary sources has a number of benefits. First, the student learns to apply the same basic principles of critical thinking in different ways with different kinds of sources. Second, the student learns valuable lessons about point of view and bias. Third, the student gets excellent experience in integrating information, a skill that will be of great value when the time comes for him or her to write research papers.

But here's the most important thing: Students are inspired to ask questions and given a way to answer the questions themselves. This is what learning is all about.

---

*Discussions and activities in this chapter prepare students to meet standards about asking and answering questions, citing evidence, and drawing inferences, CCSS.ELA-Literacy.RI.K–8.1; comparing and contrasting a firsthand and secondhand account, CCSS.ELA-Literacy.RI.4.6; interpreting visual information, drawing on information from multiple sources, evaluating the advantages and disadvantages of using different mediums, and integrating visual information with other information, CCSS.ELA-Literacy.RI.4–8.7; analyzing relationships between primary and secondary sources, CCSS.ELA-Literacy.RH.6-8.9; and comparing accounts from different sources, CCSS.ELA-Literacy.RI.K–6.9.

Differences Between Visual and Textual Sources

Many times researching any kind of primary source will lead students to a variety of sources. If, however, you are looking to create an exercise specifically to help students learn the benefits of multiple sources, we suggest a simple grouping: image, primary text, secondary text. These sources, in this order, should help you inspire curiosity in your students and give them the desire to find out more. The image presents the "mystery" and some clues. It also raises questions. The primary text—oral history, diary entry, letter, etc.—answers some of the questions raised by the image and then raises more. The secondary source answers many of the questions raised by the primary sources and, sometimes, raises others that students might want to research.

Clearly, a picture and a written account offer different kinds of information, as we mentioned when talking about Audubon's journal entry about passenger pigeons, his engraving of the bird, and the photograph taken in the 1890s. Here's our first group of three sources. This group could be used with younger students if you help them with the readings. It could certainly be used with students from the fourth grade up.

Brown Jug School students lined up along a fence outside a schoolhouse. One of the boys is wearing a cowboy hat and bandanna. Des Moines, Iowa, September 8, 1925. Wisconsin Historical Society.

First, apply the first four strategies to the photograph:

Strategy 1, this is a photograph taken of a school in Des Moines, Iowa in 1925. Strategy 2, it looks like a school portrait, taken to give to the families of the students. Strategy 3, the photographer was trying to make the class look good, and the students and teachers would have wanted to look good, too. So we can assume that they were wearing their best clothes for the occasion. Strategy 4, we can tell that this is not just one class in the school because the students are clearly different ages. There is only one teacher for all these different ages, so it's pretty safe to assume that this is a one-room school. We can't see any other buildings, so the school isn't right inside a city. It seems to be fairly warm weather, judging from the clothing people are wearing.

Here are some of the questions the photograph might raise: How does the teacher teach all these different grade levels at the same time? Can someone really get a good education in a one-room school? Why is there such a small school in the first place? Why doesn't this school combine with other schools so that they can have more teachers and more classrooms? And why is the boy standing next to the teacher wearing a cowboy outfit?*

Now, these questions can be used for a class discussion, and your students are likely to have some pretty good guesses and opinions (especially about the cowboy outfit). Then, when you're wondering what the answers to some of these questions might be, you can bring in the second source.

The second primary source is from an oral history project conducted at the Michigan City Public Library in 1977–1978. The subject of the interview is Frank McCullough, who was born in 1907.

> *Interviewer: Do you think you got a good education in the one-room schoolhouse?*
>
> *Mr. McCullough: Well, that depends. I, uh, I think that the one-room school that I had, for the most part, very good teachers and now a one-room school you could have a good education or a bad education depending on how good a teacher you had. And I think for the most part I had pretty good teachers. I remember Mary Allen was an excellent teacher.*
>
> *Interviewer Brennan: Were you kept pretty busy during the day?*
>
> *Mr. McCullough: Oh, yes. We, well, actually it was, again, up to the teacher. And the teacher could keep you very busy or not so very busy, but I think there's things about the one-room school that they have seen as an advantage even in the last few years, in... Of course, every[one] likes to bad mouth the one-room school, but it wasn't really all that bad if you had, like I said, a good teacher that could organize and really work hard and could make the classes go. Your classes run from six to eight minutes long for each class; but, for example, suppose that a fella is a pretty sharp kid, boy or girl, and you are in the third grade and you get to listen ahead as to what*

---

*These questions and others in this process hit reading standards about asking and answering questions, citing evidence, and drawing inferences, CCSS.ELA-Literacy.RI.K–8.1.

the fourth grade is doing a year before you get to it, because you got your work done fast and you listened, and then you know how to do the fractions actually a year before you get into fractions, and thing like that, so, ah...

Again, apply the first four strategies:

Strategy 1, we know that this is an oral history, an interview with a man born in 1907. Strategy 2, the purpose was to preserve some of the history of Michigan City, Indiana, and the audience was the general public. Strategy 3, there might be a certain amount of nostalgia, since many people view the events and circumstances of their childhood favorably. In Strategy 4, we learn quite a bit about a one-room school and can answer some of the questions that the photograph raised.

Can someone really get a good education in a one-room school? McCullough believes that you could get a good education in a one-room school if you had a good teacher. *How does the teacher teach all these different grade levels at the same time?* The day in his school was broken into units of six to eight minutes with different activities. If you finished what you were doing, you could listen to the lesson that older students were having and learn ahead of time.

Some of our questions remain unanswered. We still don't know why these one-room schools didn't just combine with others to make bigger schools, for example. And, of course, we will probably never know about the cowboy outfit.

The oral history excerpt also raises some new questions. If you learned the next grade's lessons, did you skip a grade? Was the school really noisy, with people doing different lessons?

Now, here is our secondary source from Iowa Pathways, a program created by Iowa Public Television.

Most one-room schools divided the day into many short periods. To keep students busy, the teacher made assignments and then called students to her desk to recite what they had learned. While a few students recited, others continued to work on their own. For example, a teacher might call up the third grade geography students for 15 minutes. She would ask them questions about what their assignment was. When they were finished, she would give them their next assignment and send them back to their desks to learn it. Then she would call up the fifth grade arithmetic students. This went on all day. At their desks students read their books or worked problems with chalk on slates. To make sure they were really working, some teachers made students read aloud to themselves. With many students reading aloud, the schoolroom could be a noisy place!

And again, the secondary source answers some questions and raises others. This is a good thing. It's this kind of dialogue among sources that not only strengthens higher-level thinking skills but promotes curiosity and gives students a genuine sense of history as a process. Historians also keep asking questions and looking for sources to answer them.*

*This exercise meets standards about reading closely, CCSS.ELA-Literacy.CCRA.R.1; asking and answering questions, citing evidence, and drawing inferences, CCSS.ELA-Literacy.RI.K–8.1; explaining events and ideas in a historical text, CCSS.ELA-Literacy.RI.4–6.3; comparing and contrasting firsthand and secondhand accounts, CCSS.ELA-Literacy.RI.4.6; analyzing relationships between primary and secondary sources, CCSS.ELA-Literacy.RH.6-8.9; and comparing texts on the same topic or accounts from different sources, CCSS.ELA-Literacy.RI.K–6.9.

Now look at these sources on child labor in cotton mills. This group of primary sources is appropriate for middle school students. The first is a photograph of a girl working as a spinner in the Vivian Cotton Mills in Cherryville, North Carolina, in 1908. The photographer was Lewis Hine and, according to his caption, this girl had been working in the mill for two years at the time this photograph was taken.

Spinner in the Vivian Cotton Mills, Cherryville, NC, 1908. Working in the mill for two years.
Photo by Lewis Hine. Library of Congress.

By reading the caption, we have gone through Strategy 1, determining what we are looking at. Strategy 2 can be accomplished by looking up Lewis Hine and discovering that he took photographs for the National Child Labor Committee. Their purpose was to expose the wrongs of child labor, and their audience was the American public. Strategy 3 uses the same information to tell us Hine's bias was the desire to end child labor in the United States. We're now at Strategy 4 and ready to discover everything we can from the image.

We see a girl who could be anywhere from 11 to 14, probably 12 or 13. She is working with heavy machinery. Her clothing and her hair have white material on them. Behind her are two boys, one of whom looks younger than she is.

But there's much that the photograph, even with its caption, will not tell us. What, specifically, is the white stuff on her clothing? And what is she doing? Is she in any danger from the huge machine she's working on? How long does she work every day? What does she get paid? Why is she working in the mill?

Now read this excerpt from an Oral History Interview with Icy Norman, April 6 and 30, 1979, in Burlington, North Carolina. The interview was conducted by Mary Murphy. Norman is describing a North Carolina cotton mill in the 1920s, about 20 years after the photograph was taken.

> *MM: Was it very dusty in the mill?*
>
> *NORMAN: Yeah, it was pretty dusty in the cotton part. That creeling job was something on cotton until they put them fans that run around the track. That would blow the lint off of it. It was terrible until they put that up there. Out there in the cotton winding room, I don't know whether they ever did get anything. Now they did on the twisters, they had them blow things on the twisters that would run around the track. That kept the lint off of the yarn. But now the winding, they'd have to stop off about twice a day and clean up in the cotton winding room.*
>
> *MM: Did people have trouble breathing sometimes?*
>
> *NORMAN: I don't know. I never did work in the cotton winding room. The only cone winding I done was on them little Universal winders. But I did work on the cotton creeling. Them fans kept it blowed. The lint, and it wasn't too linty. When the mill was stopped off and we was changing the mill or creeling a mill on it was pretty linty. But when we started it up them fans would start blowing. Then the lint would all blow off.*

Strategy 1, we know this is an oral history interview created in 1979 about Icy Norman's experience in the mills when she was young. Strategy 2, the purpose of an oral history is to preserve the stories of individuals about the past, and the audience is anyone interested in history. Strategy 3 reveals no particular bias. (If we read further in the oral history, we might discover one.) Now, for Strategy 4, we will get everything we can from the source.

Icy Norman is talking about conditions in the cotton mill. According to her, there is a lot of lint from the cotton that is being processed in the mill. That tells us what the white stuff is in the photograph. At the time that Icy Norman was working in the mills, they were beginning to put fans in some of the rooms. That suggests that there were probably no fans for the girl in the photograph, taken 20 years before. That could be something to research. The written text gives us information that we didn't get from the photograph. On the other hand, the photograph gives us a sense of the huge machinery the children were working on, which we don't get from the text.

And the questions raised? Why were these girls working in the mills? Didn't their parents make enough money to take care of them? Or did they just like making money of their own? Was it okay that all that lint was in the air? Did it make it hard to breathe? Was that huge machine dangerous to work on? Any time a student wants to know the answer to a question, you're halfway home.

And so we bring in a secondary source, an excerpt from a library research guide on the Georgia State University website.

> *Southern mill owners initially concentrated on producing coarse yarn and simple weaves because of the region's lack of skilled labor. Most Southerners had never seen a factory, much less worked in one. Mill owners used a family labor system that paid adults less than a living wage. So whole families — husbands, wives and children — labored in the mills to make ends meet.*
>
> *Mill work was a wrenching change from farm life. In agriculture the family worked cooperatively to achieve a common goal. They worked hard, but they had more control over the pace of work. In the mills, families labored for bosses who drove them hard for 10 to 12 hours a day, six days a week. The factories were noisy, hot and dangerous. Lint floated in the air and collected on the hair and skin of the mill workers. After years of working in the mills many found that the lint had also settled in their lungs. The health problems that resulted could cripple or kill them. Workers who were injured on the job lost pay and sometimes they even lost their jobs.*

The secondary source answers some of the questions raised by the primary sources. *Why were these girls working in the mills? Didn't their parents make enough money to take care of them? Or did they just like making money of their own?* According to the secondary source, the mill owners got entire families working in their mills by paying adults less than a living wage. *Was it okay that all that lint was in the air? Did it make it hard to breathe?* The lint caused serious health problems. *Was that huge machine dangerous to work on?* That question isn't answered in the secondary source. Students might have to do some research to find that information.*

A secondary source can also send your students back to the primary sources for information that might support or contradict what it says.

In the next chapter, we offer more grouping suggestions on a few different subjects. When you're creating your own groups, of course, the third source—the secondary source—will often be your textbook. You can work backwards from that to choose primary sources that will raise the questions your textbook tries to answer, or you can further research images or quotes your textbook provides and learn more about them.

---

*This exercise meets standards about reading closely, CCSS.ELA-Literacy.CCRA.R.1; asking and answering questions, citing evidence, and drawing inferences, CCSS.ELA-Literacy.RI.6–8.1; integrating visual information with other information and evaluating the advantages and disadvantages of using different mediums, CCSS.ELA-Literacy.RI.6–8.7; and analyzing relationships between primary and secondary sources, CCSS.ELA-Literacy.RH.6–8.9.

Conclusion

In looking at a grouping of primary sources, students apply basic principles of critical thinking and learn to take into account differing points of view. They also synthesize and integrate information, a very valuable academic skill. Most important, they ask questions and have the material at hand to answer those questions. In fact, they take their own journey of discovery and learning.

Things to Think About

1. How often do your students consider differing perspectives?

2. Are your students aware that there are different interpretations of the same historical event?

3. Do you think students will find it difficult to integrate information from different sources?

Cogent Quotation
The whole art of teaching is only the art of awakening the natural curiosity of young minds for the purpose of satisfying it afterwards.
—Anatole France

Chapter Ten
Apply the Strategies

As we said in the introduction, the seven strategies are not hard and fast steps in a progression. They work together. Often one strategy is so obvious you hardly know you're applying it while another is the key to completely unlocking the image or text for your students. To this point in the book, we have mostly dealt with the strategies separately and have applied them to various primary source material for you, in order to demonstrate how they work. This chapter is about giving you the opportunity to apply the strategies yourself.

We've included a variety of artifacts, images, and texts on which you can practice our seven strategies. Of course, the examples we're giving you are also designed for you to use in your classroom. With each one, you'll find some questions that could help you initiate an interesting and productive discussion.

The first group contains artifacts that can be used with both younger and older students. The second group contains single images. They may inspire research or even demand it, but we're not providing the research map and results here as we have in earlier chapters. That's up to you. The third group contains text. The readability of the text pieces varies. The first text can be read to very young students or read by early readers. Other texts have been chosen to appeal to older students. The fourth group contains groupings of images and text that will allow you to explore a topic or an event from the past using multiple sources.

In addition to the sources for all the material, we've included a URL with each image so that you can find a high-resolution electronic version online.

You'll want to apply the strategies to each of these primary sources and, after each one, we've included a few questions that you might want to include in your discussion.

The First Grouping: Artifacts

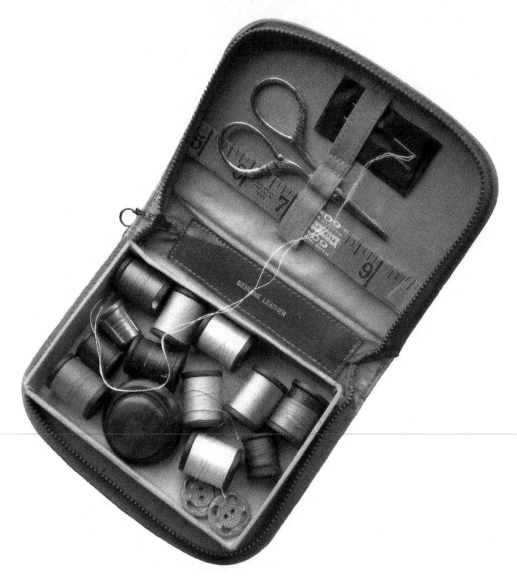

Vintage sewing kit for travelers. Austin/Thompson collection.
http://www.onehistory.org/ETEimages.htm

Some Questions:

- What is this? What are some of the individual objects contained in this?
- What was it used for?
- Have you ever done any sewing or seen anyone sew?

Rock with holes made by paddock clams. Austin/Thompson collection.
http://www.onehistory.org/ETEimages.htm

Some Questions:

- What is this?
- What shape are the holes?
- Were the holes created by a machine, a man, or an animal?

Bird's nest. Austin/Thompson collection.
http://www.onehistory.org/ETEimages.htm

Some Questions:

- What is this?
- What is it used for?
- What is it made of?

The Second Grouping: Images

Raphael Weill Elementary School, San Francisco, California, 04/17/1942. Photograph by Dorothea Lange for the Department of the Interior, War Relocation Authority. http://research.archives.gov/description/536049

Some Questions:

- Where are these children? How can you tell?
- What are they doing? How can you tell?
- How would you describe the two boys at the front of the picture?
- Do you think these boys are friends? Why do you think so?

Information to Add:

This photograph was taken in preparation for relocating the children of Japanese ancestry at this school to an internment camp.

Chippewa group building a birchbark canoe at their camp, c.1895.
Photograph by Truman W. Ingersoll. Minnesota Historical Society.
http://collections.mnhs.org/cms/display.php?irn=10464032

Some Questions:

- Where are the people in this photograph?
- What are they doing?
- How old do you think the boy on the left is?
- What does he seem to be doing?
- Can you find a picture of a finished birchbark canoe so you can understand this picture better?

Girls deliver ice. September 16, 1918. War Department Photo, National Archives.
http://research.archives.gov/description/533758

Some Questions:

- Where are these girls? How can you tell?
- What are these girls doing?
- Who do you think they were delivering ice to?
- Why do you think they're wearing overalls?
- How strong do you think you'd have to be to pick up a block of ice that big?

Information to Add:

The original caption on the photograph when it was sent out to newspapers by the United States War Department: "Heavy work that formerly belonged to men only is being done by girls. The ice girls are delivering ice on a route and their work requires brawn as well as the patriotic ambition to help."

Soybeans show the effect of the drought near Navasota, TX on Aug. 23, 2013. USDA photo by Bob Nichols.
http://farm8.staticflickr.com/7377/9679054137_ecdf8a3fbc_c.jpg

Some Questions:

- What kind of photograph is this?
- What do you think its purpose and audience were?
- How do the plants in the field look? Healthy and strong or dry and weak?
- What do you see on the ground between the rows of plants?
- Why do you think the dirt looks like that?
- What experiment could you do to see what makes dirt crack?

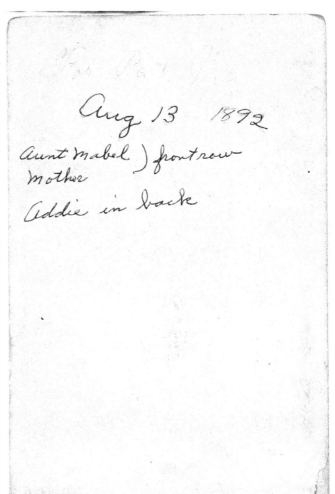

Aug 13 1892
Aunt Mabel) front row
Mother
Addie in back

Three young women. Photograph purchased from Michigan antique store. Austin/Thompson collection.
http://www.onehistory.org/ETEimages.htm

Some Questions:

- What kind of photograph is this?
- What do you think its purpose and audience were?
- Do you think these girls had any control over the photograph?
- When and where was the photograph taken?
- What do you think the relationship was of the girls to each other? Why?
- What do you notice about their clothing?
- Do the girls remind you of anyone you know?
- Is there anything in the photograph that would tell you anything about the personalities of the three different girls?

Earthrise. Apollo 11 Mission Image - View of moon limb with Earth on the horizon, Mare Smythii Region. Johnson Space Center Media Archive.
http://www.flickr.com/photos/nasacommons/5052744678/sizes/l/in/photostream/

Some Questions:

- What kind of photograph is this?
- What is its purpose and audience?
- Where was this taken?
- What does it show?
- Where do you think you could find more information about this photograph?

The Third Grouping: Texts

Diary of Laura Allis Freeman

Laura Freeman was born October 22, 1882, and lived with her family in South Royalton, Vermont. The diary was originally published in *Vermont History,* the journal of the Vermont Historical Society.

http://vermonthistory.org/images/stories/edu/GreenMountaineer/LauraFreemanDiary.pdf

January 1, 1893
Snowed pretty hard. Went and read to West a while. Lizzie is 8. Had shivered beef for breakfast & cranberry shortcakes for dinner. Skated a lot yesterday on the river with [Cousins] George, Roy, Stella and Lizzie.

January 2
Warm. West went out doors for the first time since he was taken sick...

January 4
16 below zero. Cold. Slid a lot this noon. West went outdoors a lot today. Had a written exercise in arithmetic and grammar...

January 5
Cold. Took our skates to school. Got to have compositions tomorrow. Mine is about fishing ... Not very good skating. Too much snow on the ice. Feel awfel tierd.

January 8
Very cold. All of us stayed in the house. Had rice pudding for dinner. My head aches. Don't believe I shall go to school tomorrow...

January 10
Cold. West to school. Drew the map of Europe on the board. Have finished it ... Had snow-cream for supper.

Some Questions:

- How old is Laura Freeman?
- Who do you think West and Lizzie are?
- What does Laura talk about doing?
- What do you think "snow-cream" is? How could you find out what "shivered beef" is?
- Why does Laura mention in the January 10 entry that West went to school?

Letter to Mrs. Roosevelt

Many people wrote to first lady Eleanor Roosevelt during the Great Depression. This letter was written by a teenager with a dream.
http://newdeal.feri.org/eleanor/jia0438.htm

Centerdale R.I
April 17, 1938
Dear Mrs. Roosvelt

I am writing to you to ask a big favor, the biggest favor anybody can ask. I would like to know if you would pay my way to Hollywood. You may think me crazy but I not. I mean every word I say. I know you may write back and say, lots of people ask you to pay their way to Hollywood or for some other reason, but this is different honest it is you've just got to believe in me your the only one that can help. Or you may say what can I do child. Well you could tell them that you sent me and you know I can act, I'm sure they would believe you, because you tell no fibes. Just think wouldn't you be proud if I became a great movie Star and you would say to your friends, She's the little girl who wrote to me and asked if she could go to Hollywood. And I've helped to make her a great Star. I would like to tell you all this in person and then you could see me, but I have no money for carfare and I don't want you to bother to give it to me. My Little mother is a sickly lady, she is lovely so small and sweet I love my little mother dearly and I want to help her all I can so this is why I am writing to you, It will also give me a future and bring proudness to my relatives. My Little mother has something wrong with her heart which these small Doctors dont know although they do try their best. So I thought if I went to Hollywood and earned enough money I would be able to give my Little mother the best Doctors and proper care. I am not writing this letter to Mr. Roosvelt because men don't understand things like us laides do, so I am writing to you because I know you understand. I have read and heard so many nice [missing text]

I know I can act because I make little plays which I get out of story books and act them out. ... I am fourteen years old. blue eyes, about sixty in. tall, weigh 105 1/2 pds, hair is long and curly sort of natural the color is light brown my complexion is very white. I have big eyes. Please trust in me with all your heart and I will trust in you with all my heart. Please just for my Little mother. (That's what I call her because she is so small.)

If you the Secretary should open this letter Before Mrs. Roosvelt please give it to her. Thank you.

A Little Girl who is still Unknown and Just Became Your Friend

J. I. A.

Questions:

- What do you know about the girl who wrote this letter?
- How do you think she felt when she wrote the letter?
- Does what the girl is asking make sense?
- Do you think it made sense to her?

The Fourth Grouping: Multiple Sources

Dust Bowl

FSA Photograph

Heavy black clouds of dust rising over the Texas Panhandle, Texas, March, 1936. Photograph by Russell Lee for the FSA. Library of Congress. http://www.loc.gov/pictures/item/fsa1998018489/PP/

Questions:

- What is happening in this photograph?
- What do you think it felt like to be in that car?
- What would it be like when that cloud of dust hit houses and people?

Interview: Lola Adams Crum

This interview was conducted by Brandon Case on June 23, 1998, for the Ford County (Kansas) Historical Society.

Lola Adams Crum: Well, when the dust storms really got to going, many and many a day, you see, I drove from out northwest off the farm, I drove into Dodge everyday to teach school. Many a day, I couldn't see, but one telephone post ahead of me. By the time I got to that post, I could barely see the next one, and that was day after day, I drove those six miles, just seeing one telephone post ahead of me. Sometimes, it got so bad, you could hardly see the radiator cap on the car, and I would be driving to school. Well many a day, we didn't even have school. And I can remember, my room faced the east, looked right out across the street at the neighbors, and when I could see the trees in the neighbor's yard across the street, I thought, whew boy, it's lettin' up a little. And the janitor would go down the halls and sweep out the windows, off the windowsills every hour all day long. They would just get coated with dust.

BC: How bad would it have to be before they cancelled school?

LC: Well, they, at first, when it got pretty bad, they'd cancel school everywhere . . . But, you know it happened every day and every day, and you couldn't just let school out. So they just went ahead and had school, if you could get there at all. Uh, and, then there was the "Black Blizzard.". . . On Sunday in April, 1935, and I was grading papers; sitting at our kitchen window, the window faced the north. And I looked up and there was the blackest cloud you ever saw just about a third of the way from the horizon. ... And of course, in those days, your light was a lamp, a coal oil lamp. And I reached, by the time I got into the kitchen, halfway across the kitchen; to reach for the matchbox, I couldn't see the matchbox. That dirt hit that quickly, and it just engulfed you, it just covered everything, and you couldn't see, you couldn't see anything. Now, if you wake up in the night, you can see where the window is, you couldn't tell where the window was. It was that dense. And, well, I lit the lamp, and you know, it wasn't any time between, until it seemed foggy in there. The dust had come into the room with the window shut and the doors shut.

Questions:

- What is this document?
- When was it created?
- Which of your questions about the photograph does this document answer?
- Does it raise other questions? (How did the people feel? What did they think was happening?)

Song: "So Long, It's Been Good to Know Yuh," by Woody Guthrie

Singer/songwriter Woody Guthrie wrote the song "So Long, It's Been Good to Know Yuh" about his experience during a dust storm. (Later, he wrote a different version about World War II.) There are a number of versions of the song on YouTube that you could play for your class.

Questions:

- What is this document and who wrote it?
- Does it answer any questions raised by the other documents? (What did people think was happening when they saw the dust? How did they feel?)

Things to Think About

1. What artifacts could you bring into your class? Do you think students would be interested in investigating objects more than photographs of objects?

2. What kinds of text primary sources do you think would work best with younger students? With older students?

3. How important do you think it is to use multiple primary sources?

Chapter Eleven
Find Primary Sources

In these chapters we've examined how to interpret primary sources, and we've used many examples. But we know that finding the right primary sources can be difficult. The primary sources we've shown you so far can usually be found (in high resolution) on the Internet. Most have detailed attribution and credit information. Most contain a lot of detail and information. Most can be connected to easily attainable additional research. None of that is coincidence. We spent time to find images and text that would provide the depth that would make them useful and interesting tools in your classroom. A lot of time. And we're pros.

That's why we included the previous chapter containing activities we've already researched. Our publisher, Capstone, also has materials that could be used to study primary sources. Capstone has just brought out a series of books called *First-Person Histories*, each one of which is based on a diary by a young person. Capstone's subscription site, *PebbleGo*, contains databases with content for elementary grades. The *PebbleGo* books have photographs, which can be used for analysis in the early grades.

Of course, you can also do your own research for primary sources. Finding good primary sources is possible without dedicating *all* your limited free time to the effort. In this chapter we're going to give you some suggestions for doing that.

Starting Your Search

Start with your textbooks and other educational materials. When making a good textbook, the publishers and their staff put considerable effort into finding material to complement the lesson material. They may not give you sufficient captions, credits, and attributions, but finding those for yourself just might be easier than starting from scratch. We've given quite a few examples of how this works in Chapter Seven, when discussing Strategy 5: Find more information. For the earliest grades, books with photographs that show the natural world as well as different families, communities, and societies can be used to teach basic interpretation and research skills, even those with stock photos.

If you want to go beyond your textbook or if you can't find enough information to assure yourself that the image or quoted material in your textbook is actually a primary source or has enough internal content to make it an interesting exploration, then you can do your own research.

If you've ever given your students an assignment that involves finding images, you know what happens. They go straight to Google Images. Teachers joke and tear their hair out about it. And we sympathize, but Google Images is not evil, no matter what anyone says, and it can be very useful so long as you understand what it can and cannot do for you.

Now, this might seem obvious, but Google Images is not a site of images collected by Google. It is simply part of the Google search engine. All it does is gather together the images from sites all over the Internet that relate to your search term. The fact that an image shows up in a Google Images search tells you nothing about whether it's copyrighted or, in fact, anything else of value. However, from a pure research perspective, Google Images is often a very good place to get an idea of what's out there and being used by others on the Internet. If you find an image you like, you can click on the "Visit page" button, which will sometimes lead you to the institution that owns the image. That is the place most likely to have good information about the image.

In the higher grades your students will certainly use Google Images at home to prepare history projects and papers. It's important that they be aware that many of the sites that use images (and therefore that appear in the results of a Google Images search) don't have attributions. In other words, those sites will not tell them what the images are, where they came from, who created them, and all the other information they need. Also, you can't trust that you're getting what you searched for. If you use the search term "Alexander Hamilton," not every image that shows up will be of Alexander Hamilton. If the name is on a website page and an image of someone else, say Aaron Burr, is on the same page, Google Images is likely to give you that image. So a student might illustrate a paper on Hamilton with a picture of his worst enemy.

And as a teacher, you probably won't want to use Google Images as part of a classroom research activity unless you have already carefully vetted the search term and its possible results.

There are some very good alternatives to Google, and you'll probably want to try them. First, don't forget the library. Photo books and illustrated histories are your friends. We often begin our own photographic research with a look at books of photographs. Most will have good captions and extensive photo credits. Most will use repositories beyond Corbis, Getty, and Alamy.

Then there are literally thousands of sites online that contain photographs. Fewer contain primary source text, but there are many. Stock photo houses are searchable, as are news sites such as AP Photos. Most state archives or historical societies have searchable websites of digital images from their collections. Our website www.onehistory.org contains lists of some of these state institutions. On the right side of the home page, you'll see "Get Away from Google!" Click there to see these lists.

There are also a lot of sites specifically designed to provide teachers and students with material to supplement their texts. Many of them are available only by subscription, but that doesn't mean you can't get access to them.

Subscription Sites
Text and Images

Every—or virtually every—public library now has online reference works and databases among its offerings. If you have a library card, you can use these databases. The reference works and databases each municipality chooses will be different, but it would be a good idea to check yours and see what they have to offer. Three of the most popular are listed here.

PebbleGo

http://www.pebblego.com

Capstone's subscription site, *PebbleGo,* contains databases with content for emergent readers. The *PebbleGo* books also have photographs, which can be used for analysis in the early grades.

Facts on File—History Database

This is an excellent subscription site for primary sources. Look in your local municipal library's online databases to see if they have it. It is a gateway to several separate databases, including:

- African American History Online
- American History Online
- American Indian History Online
- American Women's History Online
- Ancient and Medieval History Online
- Modern World History Online

Each of these databases has a separate section on primary sources, both image and text. These are searchable and also organized by topics. The user can also search all databases at once. The primary sources have introductory essays.

Images can be searched through the "Images and Videos" tab. The attributions for the photographs are generally quite good. In many if not most cases, the image citation tells you where to go to find the original image. The images can also be made larger.

U. S. History in Context—Gale

This site is another excellent way to find primary source text. To search for primary sources in this site, go to the search box on the homepage. There, you are given the option to search only for primary sources or only for images. As an example, a primary source search for "abolition" gave 105 results. The images on the site are less useful than on the Facts on File site, largely because many image citations refer back to a previous Gale publication rather than an original source. Also, the images cannot be made larger.

Free Sites

Text, Images, Audio, and Video

American Memory at the Library of Congress

http://memory.loc.gov/ammem/index.html

The American Memory collection contains primary source images, maps, and texts from across the Library itself as well as from places such as the University of North Carolina, Chapel Hill, and the Ohio Historical Society. One of the most important collections within American Memory is the Federal Writers' Project (FWP) slave narratives, which were recorded from 1936 to 1938.

Smithsonian Institute

http://collections.si.edu/search/

The Smithsonian Institute is enormous (963,000 online items) so basic searches can lead to huge numbers of results. However, the site allows narrowing of search terms, so you can click on "online media" and narrow your search to include only images and then go even further and click on "type" and narrow "images" to include only "photographs." For example, at the time of this writing, the search term "penguin" produced 2,414 results. Narrowing the search to only images produced 147 results. Narrowing images down to "outdoor sculpture" produced 22 results. There are options for browsing various collections as well. The site provides an excellent zoom capability for looking at details but does not have high-resolution downloads available.

National Archives

http://www.archives.gov/research/search/

The National Archives search engine is called OPA and you can get very detailed in the types of searches you want to do. It's not the easiest or most intuitive site. Use the "advanced search" option to narrow your searches to photographs or moving images or documents, etc. This is the place to go for Mathew Brady and Lewis Hine images as well as documents connected to the fight to end child labor. There is also a lesser-known series of photographs commissioned by the EPA in the 1970s, Documerica. This was a program to photographically document subjects of environmental concern in America during the 1970s and, like the FSA collection at the Library of Congress, it provides a picture of an era. As with other searches, it will be important for you to check the images to assure their appropriateness prior to sharing them with the class.

National Archives YouTube Channel

http://www.youtube.com/user/usnationalarchives

The National Archives YouTube Channel has a variety of videos, everything from a World War II era newsreel on how to recognize a Japanese Zero airplane to a half hour documentary on the Great Depression using Archive photographs and oral histories.

Digital History

http://www.digitalhistory.uh.edu/index.cfm

This excellent site provides complete lessons and resources on American history. Users can explore the site in many ways, including by topic and by era. By clicking various tabs a user can find textual primary sources, images, and teacher resources. The "For Teachers" section provides lesson plans, handouts, learning modules, and resource guides. While the lessons are probably best for high school students, many elements of the site are certainly adaptable and useful for lower grades as well.

Internet Archive

https://archive.org/

This Internet library is free and has an enormous amount of content, everything from newspapers to video to music to oral histories. The only thing not offered is images. It was founded to provide permanent access to historical collections that exist in digital format. Now the Internet Archive includes texts, audio, moving images, and software as well as archived web pages. It also provides specialized services for adaptive reading and information access for the blind and other persons with disabilities. One quick search in the audio section using the term "World War I" led to an interview with a World War I veteran made in 1968 as part of a junior high school history project.

Documenting the American South

http://docsouth.unc.edu/

This is an excellent site that contains texts, images, and audio files related to southern history, literature, and culture.

Famous Speeches in History—Audio Online—The History Channel

http://www.history.com/speeches

This section of the History Channel website has recordings of major events throughout history from the first sound recording ever made to Amelia Earhart talking about women in flight to Rodney King's statements during the Los Angeles riots. There are ads, however.

Digital Schomburg at the New York Public Library

http://www.nypl.org/locations/tid/64/node/65914

When you're looking for primary sources about African Americans, the Schomburg Center for Research in Black Culture is the place to go. There are excellent exhibits on a variety of subjects and more than 11,000 items, including prints, photographs, and historical documents on African and African Diasporan history and cultures from the 17th to the 20th centuries.

New Deal Network

http://newdeal.feri.org/

This is an excellent site containing primary source text and images on the New Deal.

Repositories of Primary Sources

http://www.uiweb.uidaho.edu/special-collections/other.repositories.html

This site provides a listing of over 5,000 websites of primary sources from around the world. This is too large to be useful for most teachers, but if you want to track down something in your state, this might be the place to go.

Image Only

Library of Congress—Prints and Photographs Division

http://www.loc.gov/pictures/

The best place to go for images, in our opinion, is the Prints and Photographs Division (P&P) of Library of Congress. Most of the images we have used in this book are from here and while not all of the images on the P&P site are available in large sizes, many are. It is easily searchable, the attributions are excellent, and the "Ask a Librarian" feature is great for additional research.

Flickr

http://www.flickr.com/

The photo sharing site Flickr is excellent, especially the section, The Commons. The Commons contains photographs from public photography archives all over the world. It includes the Library of Congress, National Archives, and Smithsonian

Institute as well as smaller institutions, such as the Mississippi Department of Archives and History and international organizations, such as the National Archives of Estonia. These institutions have not placed all of their collections on Flickr, but the sheer number and variety of institutions participating provides interesting search results. Plus you can search within The Commons collection. For example, a search using the word "holiday" resulted in an image of Ronald Reagan and Coretta Scott King at a signing ceremony for Martin Luther King Day, images of Purim and Hanukkah from the Jewish Historical Society of the Upper Midwest, and a 1939 McCall's magazine cover from the George Eastman House among many, many others. The attributions are excellent, but not all the participating institutions provide high-resolution copies the way the Library of Congress does. (Getty Images has some of its collection up on Flickr, but it is just as easy to search images directly on the Getty site.)

National Geographic

http://photography.nationalgeographic.com/photography/

National Geographic is known for its fantastic photographs. Particularly for students in the younger grades, its photographs of animals, people, and landscapes from around the world can be excellent primary sources. Sadly, some of the galleries don't have a very large number of photos, but it is definitely worth the time to check the site.

National Geographic Kids

http://kids.nationalgeographic.com/kids/

This site also has good resources for students and teachers.

Denver Public Library

http://digital.denverlibrary.org/

The Library's Digital Collection contains thousands of images of Colorado and the American West. This is a larger collection of images than the Denver Public Library images in the American Memory collection.

Metropolitan Museum of Art

http://www.metmuseum.org/ and http://www.metmuseum.org/toah/

The collections of the Metropolitan Museum of Art (the Met) contain artifacts from all parts of the ancient world. From the homepage click on "Collections." Then click on "Search the Collections." The Met also offers the Heilbrunn Timeline of Art History, which can be explored by time period, region, and theme. The Timeline of Art History is made up of 300 timelines, 930 essays, and about 7,000 objects.

Art Resource

http://www.artres.com/C.aspx?VP3=CMS3&VF=ARTHO1_3_VForm&Flash=1

This organization is a licensing house for thousands of museums and archives from around the world. In other words, it provides photographs of the art to publishers for a fee. It is not meant as a research site. However, it does contain art from so many institutions that it can be an interesting place to start a search when looking for primary sources about the ancient world. Of particular interest are the photographs on the site of archaeological digs. For example there are pictures of Tutankhamen's tomb as Howard Carter found it. Sadly, the images on this site are small and there are no free high-resolution versions available.

Bridgeman Art Library

http://www.bridgemanart.com/en-GB/

Like Art Resource, Bridgeman is also a licensing house for thousands of museums and archives from around the world and is not meant as a research site. It does represent institutions that do not have their own digitized collections, such as the Iraq Museum in Baghdad. Bridgeman has photographs of many Sumerian and Mesopotamian artifacts from the Iraq Museum, including a bust of Sargon I. There are no free high-resolution versions available, but the images display at a decent size.

Text Only

Internet History Sourcebooks Project

http://www.fordham.edu/halsall/

This site contains primary source texts from ancient to modern history, but they are largely above the K–8 level.

Gilder Lehrman Institute of American History, Primary Sources

https://www.gilderlehrman.org/collection

The Gilder Lehrman Institute is an excellent resource for anything to do with American history. It's free for students and teachers. The "Primary Sources" section provides images of the actual source as well as a typed transcription and excellent contextual information.

The University of Oklahoma Law Center: A Chronology of U. S. Historical Documents

http://www.law.ou.edu/hist/

This site provides historical documents from pre-colonial days to the present, including songs, speeches, and letters.

Science, Earth Science and Geography

National Oceanic and Atmospheric Administration (NOAA)

http://www.noaa.gov/

There are many, many parts to NOAA and its website is an excellent resource for photos and videos. However, videos and images from NOAA (the primary sources that are most relevant for a K–8 classroom and most readily available) are not organized together in one searchable database. To find videos, enter the search term "video" and choose among the various sub-agencies' pages of videos. Photographs are easier to search.

NOAA Photo Library

http://www.photolib.noaa.gov/index.html

The NOAA Photo Library gathers together many images from the sub-agencies. It contains 32,000 images, including thousands of weather and space images, hundreds of images of our shores and coastal seas, and thousands of marine species images ranging from the great whales to the most minute plankton. The Photo Library page also has a tab "Links" that connects the user to other NOAA image collections.

National Aeronautics and Space Administration (NASA)

http://www.nasa.gov/multimedia/index.html

The multimedia section of the NASA website has tabs for educators and for students, as well as links that provide access to images, videos, and NASA TV.

Lesson Plans, etc.

Library of Congress, Teachers and The Teaching with Primary Sources Program

http://www.loc.gov/teachers/ and http://www.loc.gov/teachers/tps/

These are wonderful sites on the Library's resources and on how to teach using primary sources. The main "Teachers" page" provides primary source "sets" that are searchable by grade and type of standard (Common Core, state, and organization) as well as a page that summarizes questions to ask with students, http://www.loc.gov/teachers/usingprimarysources/. "The Teaching With Primary Sources" section focuses on how to use the collections of the Library in the classroom, primarily through the *TPS Journal*, which contains excellent articles about teaching with primary sources.

TPS—Barat Primary Source Nexus

http://primarysourcenexus.org/

This is a free professional development site connected to the Library of Congress, Teaching with Primary Sources. It provides lesson ideas and plans, tips, a blog and more. There is good content for a variety of levels, but it's probably most useful for grades 5–12.

National Archives Experience—Docs Teach and National Archives Teacher's Resource

http://docsteach.org/ and http://www.archives.gov/education/

The "Docs Teach" section provides lesson plans using primary sources from the National Archives. The "Teacher's Resources" section provides links for educators. The "Special Topics and Tools" page provides links to a few National Archives e-books.

Smithsonian—Engaging Students with Primary Sources

http://historyexplorer.si.edu/PrimarySources.pdf

This is a pdf by the National Museum of American History, Kenneth E. Behring Center with lessons plans and students worksheets focusing on types of primary sources, such as photographs, newspapers, and oral histories.

Smithsonian Source, Resources for Teaching American History

http://www.smithsoniansource.org/

This site provides videos, a few lesson plans and DBQ activities in six categories, ranging from Colonial America to Inventions. It also provides links to stand-alone primary sources from the Smithsonian collection, but the site is very small and does not give the user access to all the Smithsonian's many primary source items.

Historical Thinking Matters

http://historicalthinkingmatters.org/

Through investigations into four topics (the Spanish-American War, the Scopes Trial, Social Security, and Rosa Parks), this exceptional website provides a way for students and teachers to use primary sources to develop historical thinking. It is designed to teach students how to critically read primary sources and how to critique and construct historical narratives. The site contains an overview of each subject, a road map for each student investigation, primary sources, and additional teacher resources.

Primary Source—Resources, Online Curriculum

http://www.primarysource.org/ps-world

This site provides lesson plans using primary sources about different parts of the world and world history. Most are for higher grades, but a few are specifically aimed at elementary students.

Other

Doing Internet Research at the Elementary Level

http://www.edutopia.org/blog/elementary-research-mary-beth-hertz

This is a good, basic, one-page overview of how to help focus students for Internet research.

Things to Think About

1. How would it benefit your teaching to be able to find your own primary sources?

2. Do you already use one of the sites mentioned in this chapter? What do you like about it?

3. How would it help you to broaden your knowledge of online and print resources for primary sources?

Text References

Introduction

page 11, "My dad was shell-shocked": Frances Tracy, Interview by the authors with Frances Tracy Thompson, 2000.

page 13, "21 Explicit Thinking Skills that thread": Robin J. Fogarty, PhD., "7 Critical Thinking Skills of Common Core" (Chicago: Robin Fogarty & Associates, 2012).

page 18, "Working with primary sources is specifically mandated by the Common Core State Standards": National Governors Association Center for Best Practices, Council of Chief State School Officers, *Common Core State Standards ELA* (Washington, D.C.: National Governors Association Center for Best Practices, Council of Chief State School Officers, 2010).

page 19, "The National Curriculum Standards for Social Studies addresses primary sources in": National Council for the Social Studies. *National Curriculum Standards for Social Studies: A Framework for Teaching, Learning, and Assessment* (Silver Spring, Maryland: National Council for the Social Studies, 2010).

page 19, "For example, in Florida, kindergarten students are expected to have": Florida Center for Research in Science, Technology, Engineering and Mathematics, *Next Generation Sunshine State Standards: Social Studies* (Tallahassee, FL: Florida State University).

page 19, "The Texas Essential Knowledge and Skills (TEKS) expect": Texas Education Agency, *Social Studies TEKS* (Austin, TX: Texas Education Agency, 2010).

page 20, "The California state standards say children between kindergarten and fifth grade should": California State Board of Education, *History—Social Studies Content Standards for California Public Schools Kindergarten Through Grade Twelve* (California Department of Education, 2000).

page 20, "The Ohio K–8 standards state": Ohio Department of Education, *Ohio's New Learning Standards: K–8: Social Studies* (Columbus, OH: Ohio Department of Education, 2012).

Chapter One

page 22, "When I recently asked Kevin": Sam Wineburg. "Thinking Like a Historian," *TPS Quarterly,* Vol. 3, No. 1, (Washington, D.C.: Library of Congress, 2010), http://www.loc.gov/teachers/tps/quarterly/historical_thinking/article.html (accessed November 14, 2014).

Chapter Two

page 37, "In a short time finding the task": John James Audubon, *Ornithological Biography* (Edinburgh: Adam Black, 1831), 320–321, https://archive.org/stream/ornithologicalbi01audu#page/320/mode/2up/search/Louisville (accessed November 13, 2013).

Chapter Three

page 43, "It's utterly impossible for me": Anne Frank, *The Diary of a Young Girl: The Definitive Edition* (New York: Doubleday, 1995), http://annefrank.com/about-anne-frank/diary-excerpts/ (accessed November 14, 2013).

Chapter Four

page 55, "July 28–/Went up to Uncles": Sarah Gillespie. *Diary of Sarah Gillespie: A Pioneer Farm Girl* (North Mankato, MN: Capstone, 2014), 8.

page 55, "When I write, I can shake off all my cares": Anne Frank, *The Diary of a Young Girl: The Definitive Edition* (New York: Doubleday, 1995), http://annefrank.com/about-anne-frank/diary-excerpts/ (accessed November 14, 2013).

page 55, "My name among my own people": Hamilton Holt, ed., "The Life Story of an Indian" in *The Life Stories of Undistinguished Americans as Told by Themselves* (New York: James Pott and Company, 1906), 209. https://archive.org/stream/lifestoriesundis00holtrich#page/208/mode/2up (accessed November 14, 2013).

Chapter Five

page 69, "But few men have ever existed": M. W. Delahay, *Abraham Lincoln* (New York: Daniel H. Newhall, 1939) 9, https://archive.org/details/abrahamlincoln00dela (accessed November 14, 2013).

page 72, "Father's fondness for talking": Anne Frank, quoted in Marianne MacDonald, "The things that Anne was really Frank about," *The Independent,* October 22, 1996, http://www.independent.co.uk/news/the-things-that-anne-was-really-frank-about-1359567.html (accessed November 14, 2013).

page 78, "Regarding the tenancy pictures": Nicholas Natanson, *The Black Image in the New Deal: The Politics of FSA Photography* (Knoxville: University of Tennessee Press, 1992) 4.

Chapter Six

page 89, "Rose at five": Charlotte Forten, *Diary of Charlotte Forten: A Free Black Girl Before the Civil War* (North Mankato, MN: Capstone, 2014) 6.

page 90, "U.S.S. *Maine*/Havana, Cuba": Charles Hamilton, "Letter aboard the Battleship Maine in Havana Harbor by Charles Hamilton," The Spanish American War Centennial Website, letter courtesy Monica Hamilton, http://www.spanamwar.com/mainehamiltonlet.htm (accessed November 14, 2013).

Chapter Seven

page 101, "I knew that the men were watching me": Frank B. Linderman, *Plenty-Coups, Chief of the Crows* (Lincoln: University of Nebraska Press, 1962), 30, https://archive.org/stream/plentycoupschief007810mbp#page/n43/mode/2up (accessed November 14, 2013).

page 107, "Slept in a paper box": T. H. Watkins, "Under Hoover, the Shame and Misery Deepened" in *The Great Depression: America in the 1930s* (New York: Grosset & Dunlap, 1934, 202, http://jackiewhiting.net/AmGov/Executive/Hoover.pdf (accessed November 14, 2013, see Blink's story).

Chapter Eight

page 110, "Understand that while engaged in Close Reading lessons": Sheila Brown and Lee Kappas, *Implementing the Common Core State Standards: A Primer on "Close Reading of Text"* (Washington, D.C.: The Aspen Institute, 2012) http://www.aspeninstitute.org/publications/implementing-common-core-state-standards-primer-close-reading-text#sthash.BSAjCdST.dpuf (accessed January 8, 2014).

page 113, "[B]efore I was married when I lived in Concord": Alice P. Evitt Oral History Excerpt, "Oral History Interview with Alice P. Evitt, July 18, 1979, Interview H-0162. Southern Oral History Program Collection (#4007)," Southern Oral History Program Collection, Southern Historical Collection, Wilson Library, University of North Carolina at Chapel Hill, Published by Documenting the American South, http://docsouth.unc.edu/sohp/H-0162/H-0162.html (accessed November 14, 2013).

Chapter Nine

page 119, "Interviewer: Do you think you got a good education": Frank McCullough Oral History Excerpt, "Frank McCullough. T-6-130—One Room Schoolhouse Teacher," Michigan City Public Library, Oral History Tapes, http://www.mclib.org/genealogy/oralhistory/mccoullough_f_t-6-130.pdf (accessed November 14, 2013).

page 120, "Most one-room schools divided the day": Tom Morain, "One-Room Schools," Iowa Pathways, Iowa Public Television, http://www.iptv.org/iowapathways/mypath.cfm?ounid=ob_000114 (accessed October 27, 2013).

page 122, "MM: Was it very dusty in the mill?": Icy Norman Oral History Excerpt, "Oral History Interview with Icy Norman, 1979 April 6 and 30. Interview H-36. Southern Oral History Program Collection (#4007)" in the Southern Oral History Program Collection, Southern Historical Collection, Wilson Library, University of North Carolina at Chapel Hill, 2, http://docsouth.unc.edu/nc/norman/norman.html (accessed November 14, 2013).

page 123, "Southern mill owners initially concentrated": "Work 'n' Progress: Lessons and Stories in Southern Labor History, Part III: The Southern Textile Industry," Special Collections and Archives: Southern Labor History Archives, Georgia State University, Library Research Guide, http://research.library.gsu.edu/content.php?pid=313580&sid=2576463 (accessed November 14, 2013).

Chapter Ten

page 135, "January 1, 1893/Snowed pretty hard": Laura Allis Freeman, "Diary of a Vermont Schoolgirl," Vermont Historical Society, http://vermonthistory.org/images/stories/edu/GreenMountaineer/LauraFreemanDiary.pdf (accessed November 14, 2013).

page 136, "Centerdale R.I./April 17, 1938/Dear Mrs. Roosvelt": J.I.A., Letter written to Eleanor Roosevelt on April 17, 1938, New Deal Network, http://newdeal.feri.org/eleanor/jia0438.htm (accessed November 14, 2013).

page 138, "Lola Adams Crum: Well, when the dust storms really got to going": Lola Adams Crum Oral History Excerpt, Interview: Lola Adams Crum, Interviewer: Brandon Case, June 23, 1998, Ford County Dust Bowl Oral History Project, a Kansas Humanities Council grant project, http://www.skyways.org/orgs/fordco/dustbowl/lolaadamscrum.html (accessed November 14, 2013).

Appendix One
Major Visual Collections

There are a number of photographers, collections, and themes from U.S. History that are regular fixtures among the visuals in educational materials. Here we will list how to find them yourself.

George Catlin Paintings of Native Americans

http://americanart.si.edu/exhibitions/online/catlin/highlights.html and http://collections.si.edu/search/

The Smithsonian's American Art Museum is home to George Catlin's paintings of Native Americans from the Great Plains in the 1830s. These are excellent primary source materials. His detailed portraits can be particularly rewarding for Strategy 4: Examine closely the source itself.

The Smithsonian has a site of a Catlin exhibit where you can view 34 of Catlin's paintings as well as access teacher resources. A general search of the Smithsonian collections using the term "George Catlin" results in more of the paintings. The Smithsonian's search engine provides an excellent zoom capability for looking at details. Be aware that some of Catlin's paintings contain nudity or show violent scenes such as scalpings.

Mathew Brady Civil War Photographs

http://www.archives.gov/research/search/ and http://www.loc.gov/pictures/

Mathew Brady ran a photograph studio during the Civil War, and many photographs "by" Mathew Brady might be by a different photographer who worked for him. Timothy O'Sullivan was one of the most prolific. Mathew Brady photographs from the Civil War can be found at both the Library of Congress and the National Archives. Alexander Gardner and his brother James left Brady in 1863 and went to work for the army as photographers. The "Photographic Sketch Book of the Civil War," by Alexander Gardner is part of the National Archives collection. Searching Civil War in "advanced search" limiting the search to "photographs and other graphic materials," provides 6,966 results at the time of this writing, most of which are Civil War era photographs. This is one of the collections that include images that could be disturbing to younger students.

Harper's Weekly and Other Illustrated Newspapers

Harper's Weekly, along with *Frank Leslie's Illustrated Newspaper* and the *Illustrated London News* were the major sources for visual materials as well as news articles for people in the United States and England from the mid-nineteenth until the early twentieth century. As such they are excellent sources for political cartoons, illustrations, and reportage from the era. Beware, however, that the language and imagery from this period can be extremely offensive. Also, images from *Harper's Weekly* and the other illustrated newspapers are only very rarely primary sources of the content they contain. That is not to say they cannot be valuable resources and teaching tools. They can be, but they are usually "slippery" primary sources in that they are primary sources for the thinking of the era, rather than of the event they portray.

HarpWeek (http://www.harpweek.com) is a site that features images from *Harper's Weekly* magazine. It is an excellent source for political cartoons from the era. The site isn't as user-friendly as it might be but can be worth the effort. You should check to see if your school, a local university, or municipal library has purchased the HarpWeek databases. If they have, you can have access to searchable full texts of the magazine.

The Library of Congress Prints and Photographs division (http://www.loc.gov/pictures/) contains some illustrations from Harper's as well as some from *Frank Leslie Illustrated Newspaper* and the *Illustrated London News.* None of these are in a single discrete collection. Some of the illustrations also have the contextual text as well. Doing a general search for "Harper's Weekly," for example, along with a narrowing term such as "reconstruction" is probably the best way to find content.

Editions of *Harper's Weekly* can also be found at the Internet Archive (http://www.archive.org). The archive.org site contains facsimile editions as well as searchable full-text versions. These are not perfect. They haven't been edited and contain errors. This source is only useful if you know what volume you want. *Harper's Weekly* on the Internet Archive is not really appropriate for browsing.

Solomon T. Butcher's Sod House Photographs

If there is a photograph of a sod house in one of your educational materials, then it is probably a Solomon T. Butcher photograph. As part of the American Memory program at the Library of Congress all of the 3,000 Butcher photographs were digitized. Not all are of sod houses, but all show the settlement and development of Nebraska. On American Memory, Butcher's photographs are combined with the letters of the Uriah W. Oblinger family, also from the Nebraska State Historical Society. There are, of course, many other collections of images and text about the settlement of the West including images from the Denver Public Library (http://digital.denverlibrary.org/) and images from a collection called The Northern Great Plains, 1880–1920 (http://memory.loc.gov/ammem/award97/ndfahtml/ngphome.html). This collection contains photographs of North Dakota during the period of American expansion.

Jacob Riis New York Photographs

http://collections.mcny.org/C.aspx?VP3=CMS3&VF=Home

There are photographs by Jacob Riis at the Library of Congress, but none display larger than a thumbnail outside the Library. The way to get Jacob Riis photographs is through the Museum of the City of New York. Going to the "Explore" section of the website reveals a link to the Jacob Riis collection. There is also a search function on the same page that can be used to conduct a narrower search. High-resolution versions aren't available for download, but lower-resolution versions could still be useful in the classroom.

Lewis Hine Child Labor Photographs

http://www.archives.gov/research/search/ and http://www.loc.gov/pictures/

Like the Mathew Brady photographs, the majority of the Lewis Hine images of child labor are at the National Archives and the Library of Congress. A simple search using the search term "Lewis Hine" in the National Archives search produced 1,426 results at the time of this writing, which include early child labor photos as well as Hine's WPA photographs of people during the Depression. The collection of National Child Labor Committee (NCLC) photographs taken by Lewis Hine contains the bulk of his child labor photos. Searching "Lewis Hine" in Prints & Photographs at the Library of Congress produced 5,309 results at the time of this writing, including photographs from the NCLC. The third result you get will be the NCLC collection itself, but you should ignore that, as it does not show you the images. The other results include Hine's much less well-known Red Cross photographs of World War I and people during the Depression. Frustratingly, outside the Library of Congress itself, the Red Cross photographs only display as small thumbnails.

FSA-OWI Collection—Great Depression and Domestic Activities in Early World War II Photographs

http://www.loc.gov/pictures/collection/fsa/ and http://www.loc.gov/pictures/collection/fsac/

As we noted earlier, the FSA Collection (both the black and white and the color images, which are cataloged separately) at the Library of Congress is an excellent resource for images of America—particularly rural America—during the Depression. We have not discussed that the FSA Collection became the Office of War Information in the 1940s and also contains excellent images of people involved in war work during World War II. In total the photographs cover the years 1935–1944. The project was headed for most of its tenure by Roy Stryker. It was under the aegis of the Resettlement Administration (1935–1937), then the Farm Security Administration (1937–1942), and finally the Office of War Information (1942–1944). A simple search using the terms "war" and "factory" produced 1,243 results at the time of this writing, many of which were women working in war industries. The FSA-OWI Collection also contains many photographs of the relocation of people of Japanese ancestry and their lives in internment camps.

National Archives - War Relocation Authority Photographs

http://www.archives.gov/research/search/

For more photographs of Japanese internment during World War II, go to the National Archives and locate the "Central Photographic File of the War Relocation Authority." This series contains 3,960 items at the time of this writing. You can search within the series as well. For example, a search within the series using the term "Manzanar" produced 481 images of people living in the Manzanar camp.

Appendix Two
A Brief History of Image and Sound Technology

People have been writing down their thoughts for over 4,000 years. So if a text purports to be a Sumerian poem from, say, 2030 B.C., it's a possibility. The same is not true with imagery. A cave painting might have been created 40,000 years ago, but a photograph of that painting could only have been taken within the last 150 years. Today many documentary films use reenactments to help illustrate the history they are communicating. Your students may not be aware that there was no film during the Civil War. Knowing the history of photography, film, and audio will help you help your students identify whether a visual or auditory source could in fact be a primary source at all.

Photography

All early photographs were black and white, although some were colorized or had paint added to them. The first photograph was taken in 1826. Daguerreotypes were invented in 1839. Ambrotypes came into use in the mid-1850s. Gradually, after 1860, photographs on paper became more common. The exposure time required in the earliest photographs was very slow, up to 30 minutes! Exposure times were quickly reduced but could still be as long as one minute. In 1877 a faster shutter was invented so exposures could be as fast as 1/25th of a second. This made motion photography possible. George Eastman invented the Kodak camera, and it went on the market in 1888. It cost $25.00, not a small sum at the time. The Brownie camera was invented in 1900. It was small, easy to hold and carry, and cost only $1.00. In 1930 reliable flashbulbs become available, and in 1935 color film (Kodachrome) started being sold. In 1947 the Polaroid camera was invented. Into the 1950s, color film was still not common. Use of color film for most people's snapshots did not become common until the mid-1960s. The first point-and-shoot camera, the Instamatic, was introduced in 1963.

Film

Motion pictures were not invented until the 1890s and initially there was no sound. The first stories on film were not made until 1903. The first cartoon was made in 1906. The first newsreel was not made until 1911. Sound did not become part of film until 1927. Color was introduced in 1935. Home movies were not really even possible until the invention of 16 mm film in 1923, but the equipment was far too expensive for any but the wealthiest people. By the 1930s, 8 mm film had been invented. The film and equipment became cheap enough by the 1950s that home movies were far more common. The first video camcorder was introduced in 1980.

Audio

A way to record sound was not invented until 1877. The gramophone was invented 10 years later. Some of the first examples of sound recordings being made for documentary purposes occurred between 1906 and 1908. When he was running for governor of New York in 1906, William Randolph Hearst recorded his speeches for distribution. In 1908 the musicologist John Lomax recorded a man singing "Home on the Range." By 1917 jazz and blues records were being made and soon record sales went into the millions. In 1918, the use of sound recording to document history was introduced when William Gaisber recorded artillery exploding on the battlefield. The technology for magnetic tape recording was developed in the early 1930s.

At Maupin House by Capstone Professional, we continue to look for professional development resources that support grades K–8 classroom teachers in areas, such as these:

Literacy	Language Arts
Content-Area Literacy	Research-Based Practices
Assessment	Inquiry
Technology	Differentiation
Standards-Based Instruction	School Safety
Classroom Management	School Community

If you have an idea for a professional development resource, visit our Become an Author website at:
http://maupinhouse.com/index.php/become-an-author

There are two ways to submit questions and proposals.

1. You may send them electronically to:
   http://maupinhouse.com/index.php/become-an-author

2. You may send them via postal mail. Please be sure to include a self-addressed stamped envelope for us to return materials.

Acquisitions Editor
Capstone Professional
1 N. LaSalle Street, Suite 1800
Chicago, IL 60602